COMMUNI-CATION

KEY TO YOUR TEENS

NORMAN WRIGHT
REX JOHNSON

HARVEST HOUSE PUBLISHERS
Eugene, Oregon 97402

COMMUNICATION—KEY TO YOUR TEENS

Copyright © 1978 Harvest House Publishers
Eugene, Oregon 97402
Library of Congress Catalog Card Number: 78-61872
ISBN #0-89081-158-X

CONTENTS

INTRODUCTION

Are you finding that raising teenagers isn't all it's cracked up to be? The kids who used to be so close now want to be left alone to do their own thing. And you know some of their plans are going to bring them trouble.

Maybe you've had the traumatic experience of being informed that your teenager was just arrested. Or worse, maybe you're in the unenviable position of hoping he or she won't be arrested though you suspect your teenager has broken the law.

Perhaps you're one of those few fortunate parents who enjoy the friendship of their teens. You enjoy being with them and what's more, they enjoy being with you. Sure, they're not perfect, but neither are you. Great!

Whether raising teens is for you a joy, a mixed blessing, or a heartache, this book suggests ways you as parents can build positive relationships with your teens. Obviously, the way your teens behave today is directly related to the relationship you have been developing since they were babies. But that isn't the whole story. If it were, this book would have been titled, "Infant Communication—Key To Your Teens."

What **you** say and do can alter a poor relationship. The ways you change will have an effect on your teens. You can "turn over a new leaf." But if your present relationship with one or more of your teens is already positive, be thankful and keep on building.

In order to help you enrich your relationship with your teens, this book should be tried, not just read.

6/COMMUNICATION—KEY TO YOUR TEENS

As you thumb through the book, you'll notice two kinds of response sections in each chapter. The **"What do you think?"** sections invite you to think and then write out your responses to questions dealing with what you've read. If you stop and respond in writing before you go on, you'll find your reading more helpful and rewarding.

WHAT DO YOU THINK?

What might be some benefits of an enriched relationship with your teenage son or daughter?

1. _____

2. _____

3. _____

The **"What is your plan?"** sections challenge you at the end of each chapter to try some of the ideas to see how they might work for your family. You'll find that putting ideas to work will make them much easier to remember.

The best way to use this book is to make it a family project. Introduce to your teens the compansion book to this one (It's title is **Communication—Key To Your Parents**). Ask them to read and respond to that book at the same pace you read this book and you will find that you have plenty of good things to talk about together. You might even try a weekly "family council" based on your reading and responses.

I'd like to recommend two more books you or your teens might be interested in. **Building Positive Parent-Teen Relationships** is a teacher's guidebook for a class or seminar on parent-teen relationships. You might suggest it to your pastor, youth minister or Sunday school teacher. You might even use it yourself to lead a small group of families in building positive parent-teen relationships. It is authored by the writers of this book and published by Harvest House Publishers.

An Answer to Family Communication is a book to enrich your own marriage or to help others enrich theirs. Its author is Norman Wright, and it is also published by Harvest House.

CHAPTER I

You and Your Family

Every two or three weeks, it seems, one of **those** days would happen. It started out wrong, went wrong, and finished up leaving Bob wondering which way was up.

It wasn't a job problem. Bob was never threatened by problems at work. He expected problems at work but he knew how to deal with them. He had been trained both in college and by his company to solve problems in his business. But when **those** days came around it was even difficult to solve problems at work.

It wasn't a health problem. Bob was in good shape for his age and had lots of energy. He wasn't depressed, an alcoholic, or even overweight. But when **those** days came around he felt anxious all day and totally drained by bedtime.

It wasn't a spiritual problem. Bob was an active member of a strong Bible-believing church. He had a growing relationship with Jesus, was teaching an adult Sunday school class, and involved in a weekly growth group. But when **those** days came along, Bob felt spiritually demoralized.

It was a family problem. With almost calendar regularity Bob had to deal with problems created by one of his family members—usually one of his teens. Those days were crisis days. Everything usually ran all right except on **those** days.

Bob's family was not breaking up. His teens were not in trouble with the police or at school. Bob was handling life quite successfully. His family was even a source of pleasure to him—except, of course, on **those** days.

So when a course on "Parent-Teen Relationships" was offered by his church, Bob and his wife Nancy, along with their two teenagers, Jim and Janice, enrolled. They weren't desperate for help, but they wanted the "family enrichment" that the course offered. Bob didn't mention it, but he wanted to find some better ways to cope with **those days**.

WHAT DO YOU THINK?

1. **Is enriching your family life one of your interests? If so in what areas do you sense a need? Check the topics that especially interest you.**

    Family strengtheners_____
    Home atmosphere _____
    The role of parenting_____
    Trusting your teenagers_____
    Problem teenagers_____
    Communication with teenagers _____
    Creative conflict _____
    Dealing with emotions _____
    Your expectations and theirs _____
    Your teenagers' friends_____

2. **Now please put an "S" next to each item in num-**

ber 1 which you think would especially interest
your spouse.
3. You might add your teenagers' names next to the
   items they would be interested in.

Hopefully this book, like a course in Parent-
Teen Relationships, or maybe along with such a
course, will provide the resources you're looking for
to enrich your family life.

ADOLESCENCE = ALIENATION?

One of the characteristics of a family in which
there are adolescents is changing family relationships. This is natural and is something young parents
can look forward to experiencing. In fact, if a
parent's relationship with his or her teenager is the
same when the teenager is eighteen as it was when
he was thirteen, something is wrong. Neither the
parents nor the teenager have grown.

However many parents and teenagers fear adolescence because they equate changing relationships
with alienation. In their view adolescence is the time
to expect rebellion, maybe embarrassment, a frac-
turing of family relationships, and deep hurts. Does
it have to be this way? Time and again, the young
parent is cautioned to expect trouble when his or her
children become teenagers. One envisions "The
Music Man" singing "Oh you've got trouble—with a
capital T—and that stands for Teenagers!

But just because relationships change doesn't
mean that they have to get worse. To parents who
have everything in control with a fifth grade boy or
girl, the thought of having to cope with teenagers
they can't spank is threatening. But control is not the

only factor. Growing independence can also bring growing self-discipline. A growing self-identity can be accompanied by growing love (more mature love than a child's love) for parents. A growing value system can produce growing relationships at home as well as away from home.

FOR THE ENROUTE FAMILY

Young parents whose oldest child has not yet entered Junior High can establish patterns of communication early that will certainly be helpful as their children become teenagers. They will still face problems with their teenagers, but good communication and conflict resolution patterns will reduce the severity of most of the problems, eliminate some altogether, and allow for healing to come easily when it's needed.

But what about the family who already has one or more teenagers—the enroute family? Is it too late to establish good patterns of communication? We say, "No!" Even if your last teenager is approaching twenty and you've always had very little communication you can still begin the healing-building process. But you as a parent must take the initiative, and two ingredients must both be present and active— willingness to change and willingness to work.

In Mark 10, some Pharisees asked Jesus about the legality of divorce. Jesus asked them what Moses had commanded, and they replied accurately. Then Jesus told the Pharisees why God had given Moses the divorce laws, "Because of the hardness of your heart he wrote you this commandment" (KJV). Jesus in this statement implied the ingredients that bring healing to a marriage, even a poor marriage.

The same ingredients can bring healing to parent-teen relationships. What did He mean by "the hardness of your heart?"

A spiritual, emotional, and relational hard heart is just like a physical heart that has gotten hard. Physically, we call it hardening of the arteries. The heart won't work like it was designed to and it's ability to change is restricted. We then find all sorts of reasons not to invest the time, energy and resources into people that are needed to make a relationship develop. After all, we're right, aren't we?

But what if we parents are willing and ready to change and our teenagers are not? Are parents to throw out their system, their way of life, their relationships with their teenagers and with their friends to redevelop a relationship with a rebellious teenager?

We have in Scripture a father who faced just such a dilemma. Luke 15:11-32 does not say that this father's two sons were teenagers but they both behaved like many teenagers do today. The younger son demanded his share of his father's estate and in a few days took off.

WHAT DO YOU THINK?

1. **If you had been the father would you have given in to your son's demand for his share of the estate?**

   Why or why not?

The father in this parable could have simply denied his son's request. He might have given him a part of his inheritance, saving the rest for later. He might have given his son the money but then somehow kept him from leaving. Or, as so many parents do, he might have gone after his son to rescue him from his evil friends and saved his money. There are probably other options he might have taken, but he didn't.

In dealing with his rebellious son, this father did not throw out his value system, his way of life, or his relationship with the rest of the family. Some might say that he was an awfully permissive father and made a mistake giving his son all that money. But notice some details about this parable.

Jesus told the parable to teach us about God's way of dealing with His people. The father in this parable is a picture or type of God. So the way the father dealt with his sons is a picture of the way God deals with us, His children. The parable also becomes a model to us parents as we deal with our children.

First, the father let his son go. Sometimes, parents have to let their children go. They will make mistakes, they will waste a lot of money, and they may hurt themselves in many ways. But some people only learn "the hard way." The question is, do we as parents value the individuality, autonomy and responsibility of our teens, like God values ours? Or must our teens be carbon copies of us?

The father in the parable was gracious, not permissive. A permissive father would have given his son the money and let him go. But he would have done so simply to get his son out of his hair. A permissive father would not have staged a celebration upon the return of his son. Why add a fatted calf to the rest of his losses?

The father in the parable was patient, too. He was patient enough not to chase after his son when he left. He was patient enough not to intervene even during the famine. He was patient enough to wait till his son truly "came to his senses." In the end he was patient enough not to demand an apology but to wait for his son to demonstrate repentance through changed behavior.

The father in the parable was a forgiving person. He had a lot of money as well as time, love and reputation invested in his son, and now all that investment was gone! Yet the father could forgive enough to trust his son with the family ring! That ring was like a credit card is today. It was used to seal documents. He could not have trusted his son that much without forgiving him.

The father in the parable was faithful to his rebellious son. He was so "full of faith" that he went ahead and gave his son the money, let him go, let him squander the money, and took his repentance at face value when the son came back. God's faithfulness to us is a worthy model for our relationship with our teenagers.

Many parents would say, "When it comes right down to it, I could not be as gracious, as patient, or as faithful as the father in the parable. I cannot forget all the other values involved, either. What was good enough for my older son is good enough for my younger one as well." But these are the very attitudes and values we are called upon by Scripture to change. As "enroute parents," even successful ones, we are challenged by Scripture to become more conformed to the image of Christ than we already are. Needed change, then, is not a function of previous success, nor something only for our teenagers.

In our culture a man who is noted for his success is not called upon to change very much—he is already successful. In our relationship with God it is only the immature Christian who senses no need to change. The more we grow in Christ, the more we recognize how much more growth is available.

TWO-WAY ACCOUNTABILITY

When we parents change and grow we show our teenagers by our lives that it is all right for them to change and grow. In fact, one of the best ways we can restructure our relationships with our teenagers to help them is to begin building two-way accountability. What is two-way accountability? Let's look at its opposite to help define it.

The world's way of structuring relationships is on a series of one-way accountability relationships making up a line of authority. At the bottom is the guy who is accountable to his boss who is in turn accountable to his boss all the way up the ladder to the top of the system. The president or manager may be accountable to a board, and in some companies there is a profit-sharing program that makes the president indirectly accountable to lower level employees.

One-way accountability is the system most families are familiar with. Kids are accountable to adults, especially parents, but not vice-versa.

What if a dad went to his teenage son and said, "Son, I'm working on learning to not be so anxious and to commit everything to God in prayer. I'd like to report my progress to you each evening, and I'd like you to ask me how I'm doing. I'd like you to suggest ways I can learn quicker when you think of them, and when you notice me getting anxious about something, I'd like you to remind me to commit right then, O.K.?"

WHAT DO YOU THINK?

1. **What are 2 or 3 things that might happen if a dad tried the above idea?**

   a. _____

   _____

   b. _____

   _____

   c. _____

   _____

2. **How would your teenagers react, in the long run, to two-way accountability?**

   _____

The initiation of two-way accountability **by a parent**, sets the stage for several things to happen: 1) Teenagers have a model for change that will make change and growth easier to accomplish; 2) Teenagers have a model for voluntary accountability which if they develop will increase their self-discipline and responsibility greatly; 3) Parent-teen communication can become more adult-to-adult rather than adult-to-child.

PARENTS SET THE PACE

When adults first become parents they have to learn a new role—the role of parenting. As parents they are totally responsible for their baby's welfare. Then, after many years of coping with this role, parents are called upon to give it up. Their children are now adults and may even have families of their own. Giving up a role that has been a part of one's life for some twenty years or more, is not easy. Some parents can never give it up—and the most common result is in-law problems.

Parents who can anticipate the day they will have to trade in their role of parenting for some new roles can make the whole process easier on themselves and their teenagers. At the same time, they encourage adult behavior in their teenagers. When a parent initiates two-way accountability, he, in effect, says, "As one adult to another, I need your help. I know you're not totally adult yet, but you're not a child either. I'd rather encourage your growth toward adulthood than try to hang on to you as a child."

The objection some parents (and teenagers) might have to this idea is that we are forcing kids to grow up in a hurry. But most parents appreciate and enjoy maturing teenagers, whatever their age. This can be a reality if parents are willing to set the pace.

WHAT IS YOUR PLAN?

1. If possible, spend some time with your spouse, maybe an afternoon and evening date, discussing the quality of your relationship with your teenagers in light of the following questions:

    a. Are our teenagers more or less mature than peers of their own age? How do we know?

    b. Are our teenagers more or less mature than we would expect them to be for their age? How do we know?

    c. Do our teenagers have, in us, models of growth in the areas of life in which we would like them to grow?

    d. What areas of growth in our lives would lend themselves to establishing two-way accountability with our teenagers?

CHAPTER II

What is a Good Parent?

"Anyone who has an adolescent child, or even well remembers his own adolescence, knows that it is only slightly facetious to say that in some sense the period of adolescence is, itself, a "developmental psychosis." Laurence Finberg, M.D., Albert Einstein College of Medicine.

"A parent cannot change a nearly grown child—he can change only himself and his reaction to the child. Often the most helpful thing the parent can do is to stop trying to change the youngster. It can't be done anyway and the parents' effort can stand in the way of the adolescent's changing himself." Families Anonymous.

"I could be with a president or the Pope and enjoy it, of course, but being with my son, Bill, gives me a particular pleasure that surpasses all that by far." Comedian Steve Allen.

"The home remains crucial for teenagers. Sometimes parents feel that their teenagers act and talk as if the home didn't matter much except as a refueling base. The truth of the matter is that it is in this period when youth particularly need the accepting, sustaining, limiting influences of the family structure." Atlee Beechy.

"Good families take work." Howard Hendricks.

Which of the above quotes do you think is the best description of being a parent? Maybe you have a quote of your own to add to the list.

When a couple have their first baby they very proudly say, "I am a father," or "I am a mother!" Everybody understands that they have had a baby. And all who have had children of their own know a lot of changes are coming for the young couple. They have taken on the responsibility of parenting. When the "new daddy" comes to work a week later cross-eyed from lack of sleep we say "now you **know** you're a father."

But parenting is not just having babies. Many parents never had any babies. They adopted children. And many couples who had a baby gave it up for adoption. So what is parenting? However we might define it, parenting for most parents is a role. That means it is learned and molded by the culture the parents grew up in. When parents change their roles or step out of them while interacting with their children, everybody's expectations are shocked.

The role of parenting is learned; not formally in a school or church setting, but by imitation and absorption. It might be helpful if the study of parenting were a part of more churches' educational programs. Maybe more homes would be "Christian homes." (More will be said about this in chapter 12.) But most parents relate with their children pretty much the way their parents interacted with them. Those who don't tend to relate in patterns opposite to the ways their parents interacted with them. They learned this from their parents, too.

For instance, the parent who is "authoritarian" in his interactions with his children usually had an "authoritarian" father himself. But many parents who are quite permissive with their children also had "authoritarian" parents. They have reacted to their parents' strictness with a determination not to repeat the "mistakes" their parents made.

The idea that the role of parenting is molded by culture becomes more obvious when we compare the expectations parents in different cultures have of their teenagers. In some cultures a teenager wouldn't think of even questioning his father's word. In our culture a teenager is rebellious almost by definition. In many cultures a father is expected to teach his son his vocation. In our culture a teenager might not pick his vocation until he's well into college and in his twenties. In some cultures parents pick their teenagers' bride or groom. In our culture parents might not even meet their teenagers' bride or groom till just before or even after their wedding.

The role of parenting is inclusive; parents are expected to act like parents. Even divorced parents are expected to maintain an interest in, and support of their children. It's the expectation that parents act like parents that makes parenting a role.

When parents get used to playing their role a certain way they become comfortable with their role and tend to avoid changing it. In fact, they may continue to interact with their children as children even when the children have become adults, are married and have children of their own. Many parents also interact with people outside their family from the perspective of their role as parents. They try to be their co-workers' or friends' conscience, authority, decision-makers, etc.

How we parents play our roles is so varied in our society that many extremes have developed. When parents play these extreme roles, problems are created for our teenagers. The irony is that these extreme roles are usually played by parents because we are trying our best to be good parents! When we are playing these extreme roles, we don't see ourselves as extreme. We can identify other extremes, but we don't recognize our own extremes.

What are the extreme roles in question: Let's discuss them one by one. [1]

PERFECTIONISTIC—COULD NOT CARE LESS

The perfectionistic parent is never satisfied with the job he's doing as a parent or with his teenagers. If his teenagers' grades in school are "Bs" he feels they should have been "As." If the grades were all "As" except one B or C he puts pressure on his teenager to bring up the low grade rather than being thankful for such outstanding work in the other classes. No boyfriend is good enough for his daughter; no girl is good enough for his son. Even when his son or daughter wins a first place this parent may not be satisfied: "He should have won by a wider margin."

Many perfectionistic parents inhibit most of their emotions, and find it hard to relax. Being in control at all times is important to them. They teach their kids the same values with such statements as "Big boys don't cry" and "keep a stiff upper lip."

At the other extreme is the parent who is always satisfied and disinterested in relationship to his teenagers. This parent's central concern in comfort for himself—whatever his teenagers do or don't do is their concern, not his. Like the perfectionistic, he rarely encourages his teenagers, not because they can't do well enough to suit him, but because it doesn't matter to him how well they do. Whether they get "Cs" or "As" at school is of little consequence to him. In fact he probably couldn't say what grades his teenagers get—he doesn't know. He rarely if ever supports his teenagers in their sports or other activities, and it doesn't matter to him who their friends are. Time spent with his teenagers is at his own convenience and with his interests. He doesn't dislike or reject his teenagers, he's just too selfish to care.

REJECTING—ACCEPTING

The rejecting parent seems not even to want his teenagers around him. He makes excuses to be away from his family. He is not a perfectionist nor is he disinterested. He resents his teenagers. Many rejecting parents feel trapped by their family. They blame their lack of success on having to take care of their children.

Some parents reject their teenager because they cannot accept the lifestyle the teenager has chosen. It differs from their own and they cannot tolerate someone around them whose values have become so different from theirs. Everything the teenager does begins to symbolize rebellion and it becomes difficult for these parents to see their own teenager as a person.

It is helpful to notice how God reacts when we rebel against His values. "All of us like sheep have gone astray, each of us has turned to his own way; but the LORD has caused the iniquity of us all to fall on Him" (Isaiah 53:6). Instead of rejecting us, God has reconciled us to Himself by Jesus' death on a cross.

It's been said that it is better to give than to receive. It's also easier to give than to receive. The accepting parent wants to be with his teenagers and wants them to be with him. He chooses to enter their world as well as to invite them into his. If they are interested in soccer, he goes to their games and even practices with them when they let him. He does this even if he would prefer baseball or basketball.

Accepting parents can initiate love and affection, and can also accept it. They are not embarrassed by displays of affection in public. Teenagers can talk with accepting parents without fear of being ostracized or rejected.

Being accepting parents does not mean that these parents accept or approve of wrong behavior, attitudes or values. They don't condone sin. But they continue to love, accept, and believe in their teenagers even when a wrong has been committed.

OVERPROTECTIVE—UNDERPROTECTIVE

Overprotective parents cannot trust their teenagers. Actually, they cannot trust themselves—especially the job they have been doing as parents. They mean well, and love their teenagers very much—so much that they fail to distinguish between doing things **with** their teenagers and doing things **for** them.

It is especially easy in our culture for parents to be overprotective with their daughters. Most parents want to be consulted on the dating decisions their teenagers make. But overprotective parents want to choose their teenagers' dates for them. These parents also set unrealistic limits, often imposing them without allowing their teenagers to develop responsibility by being involved in the limit-setting process.

The consequences of overprotectiveness are usually that teenagers learn conformity but not responsibility. Sometimes overprotected teenagers learn deception, appearing to conform, while at the same time doing their own thing.

Underprotective parents believe so strongly in the "School of hard knocks" that they fail to support and encourage their teenagers when support and encouragement are appropriate. They are like the dad in the song who named his boy "Sue" so he would have to learn to defend himself.

WHAT DO YOU THINK?

1. **Please place an 'X' on the line representing where you think you are on a continuum between very perfectionistic and very careless.**

1	2	3	4	5	6	7	8	9	10

   Perfectionistic   Careless

2. **Please add an "S" to the line where you think your spouse would mark you.**
3. **Please add the first letter of each of your teenager's names where you think they would place you.**
4. **Draw your own lines on a separate sheet of paper and follow steps 1-3 for a rejecting—accepting continuum and an overprotective—underprotective continuum.**
5. **Discuss these continuums with your spouse and then with your teenagers, unless you find**

communication difficult. If so, wait till after chapter ten and then discuss this chapter.

OVERINDULGENT—STINGY

Overindulgent parents give their children everything but themselves. Their way of expressing their love to their teenagers is to buy them a gift. Frequently they are caught in a vicious cycle: To express their love they buy gifts—including a bigger home, cars, clothes, vacations, etc. To pay for all these gifts they have to work more which takes them away from home more. This causes guilt feelings which they reduce by buying more gifts.

Usually these parents and their teenagers are blind to their overindulgence. It's a pattern that started well before the kids were teenagers. Overindulgence is bad for the teenagers as well as enslaving to the parents. It tends to develop teenagers who are selfish and demanding and whose attitude is that the world owes them a living.

Stingy parents, on the other hand put their own interest ahead of their teenagers. They are still learning the meaning of possession themselves, and material possessions become symbols of self-worth. These parents have often had such a hard time attaining their present lifestyle and possessions that thrift has become a rigid habit. They find it extremely difficult if not impossible to use their resources for any kind of recreation or enrichment.

The parent playing this role plays it with the excuse that he's saving for his family. The irony is that they probably won't benefit from it until their parents' death. Then they may be too bitter to appreciate it.

OVERPERMISSIVE—LEGALISTIC

Overpermissive parents are afraid of stifling their teenagers' creativity, personality, or future. Some overpermissive parents are simply afraid of asserting themselves. They may not like what their teenagers are doing, but they have not learned how to say "No," how to communicate their feelings, or how to care enough to confront.

The parent who is a legalist is usually insecure about confronting his or her teenagers and about making decisions that involve them. But instead of withdrawing or giving in to avoid conflict, the legalist allows a code, a set of rules, or some outside authority to make all the decisions. The outside authority may be a grandparent, a neighbor, a church, or even a book on parent-teen communication.

Legalistic parents are especially concerned about being "right" in their role of parenting and feel anxious when there is no precedent governing a situation. Their teenagers tend to displace their frustrations with their parents onto the code their parents are using and reject the code.

SEVERE—TRUSTWORTHY

The severe parent is totally unpredictable. When he or she is happy all is well and life is enjoyable for all who are present. But when a severe parent gets angry or frustrated he or she gets violent. This violence may take the form of shouting or it may even become physical violence such as beating. The severe parent lacks control over his impulses and fails to distinguish between punishing and discipline. Alcohol or drugs are often a major part of the severe parent's life, but they are not the cause of his problems—just the well-worn excuse. The severe parent needs help in coping with his own feelings before he'll be able to cope with his relationships successfully.

Trustworthy parents, on the other hand, can handle frustrations and anger. They are secure enough to trust others as well as themselves. They are marked by their ability to forgive. They can be vulnerable by choice and are more objective than subjective or arbitrary. We will discuss trustworthiness in greater detail in chapter three.

WHAT DO YOU THINK?

1. As you did with the first three continuums, rate yourself in the areas of overindulgent—stingy, overpermissive—legalistic, and severe—trustworthy. Then predict how your spouse would rate you in each, and how each of your teens would rate you. Verify your ratings and predictions with them if you're ready to.

2. If you tend to be overindulgent, can you think of some things you could do with your teenagers for their next birthday instead of giving them a store-bought present? Jot down some possibilities here.

3. If you tend to be legalistic, can you think of three

or four rules that have outlived their usefulness? If so, what are they? Jot them down here.

4. **If you tend to be severe, maybe your idea of parenting needs rethinking. From whom did you learn how to parent? Maybe you didn't have the best teacher. If not, who could you watch and learn from?**

INCONSISTENT—CONSISTENT

Inconsistent parents interact with each other and with their teenagers on the basis of the mood they are in at the time. A request to go to a friend's house will sometimes get a cheery ''sure.'' Other times the same request will get a lecture on laziness, on being inconsiderate, on responsibility, or any of a dozen other topics. As the parent's mood changes the rules change and values are unpredictable.

The inconsistent parent differs from the severe parent in that he is far less violent. Sometimes he or she is overpermissive, too, but not consistently so. He tends to make decisions from a self-centered point of view, usually without considering implications for other people. As teenagers grow in independence they learn not to depend on an inconsistent parent. So, rather than learning interdependence, alienation is usually the result of a parent's inconsistency.

Consistent parents are not computers, but they live by a set of values and most of their decisions are predictable. This does not make them legalistic or boring. They are stable and usually quite self-disciplined. They have good and bad moods too, but their moods don't determine their decisions or their relationships. No human is ever 100% consistent. In fact a person trying too hard to be consistent is in danger of relating to people (including himself) as objects rather than as persons. People become either all good or all bad. The defects in "good" people and the good qualities in "bad" people are consistently denied. The parent who is not overly consistent, though, is easier for a teenager to relate with than the parent who is inconsistent.

DOUBLE-BINDING — ENABLING

Did you ever have someone say something to you like, "Go have fun with your friends. I'll stay here and be happy doing the dishes by myself"? You feel guilty if you go because you know that the only thing worse than washing the dishes is washing and drying them alone. You feel guilty if you don't go because your friends were expecting you and because you let yourself be manipulated into staying.

Double-binding is a way to maintain control over people by playing upon their guilt feelings. The double-binding parent gives his teenagers a choice, but they are so structured that the teenager is bound to feel guilty, no matter which choice he makes. The double-binding parent typically plays the role of martyr so that the teenager feels depended upon.

Actually, double-binding is a way to keep one's teenagers dependent. Teenagers learn not to make choices or be assertive or to bring requests to their parents. They eventually cut off communication.

Enabling parents invest in their teenagers' present and future. They help their teenagers learn how to choose by supporting many of their choices even when the teenagers' choices are not the best ones. They enable their teenagers to become responsible by trusting, disciplining, forgiving, challenging, and encouraging them. They give their teenagers the freedom to be themselves while giving them love, direction, and a pattern to follow. When their teenagers choose not to follow the pattern, they honor that choice while praying for their teenager and being available to help him or her out of a jam.

FAULTY MODEL—GODLY MODEL

Faulty models are parents whose behavior teaches their teenagers illegal, unethical, or sinful ways of behaving. At the extreme are criminal parents. But lots of Christian parents are also faulty models at a less extreme level. Parents who cheat on income taxes, fish without a license, make promises they don't keep, etc. are teaching their kids by example how to cheat, steal, or lie as long as they are not caught.

Since so much of a teenager's way of life is absorbed or caught from his parents, it is important to have parents who are Godly models. Godly models are parents who realize that the way their teenagers will understand God is on the basis of the teenagers' relationships with their parents. They are not playing God for their teenagers, they are representing God to their teenagers as best they can. So God's attributes are important to them, and being conformed to the image of Jesus (Ephesians 4:13) is a way of loving their teenagers as well as a way of following Jesus. They teach by the way they live.

WHAT DO YOU THINK?

1. As you did with the first six continuums, rate yourself in the areas of inconsistent—consistent, double-binding—enabling, and faulty model— Godly model. Then predict how your spouse would rate you in each, and how each of your teens would rate you. Verify your ratings and predictions with them if you're ready to.

2. What is your teenager's idea of God? Do they focus on His justice and judgement, His forgiveness, His faithfulness, His love? If you're not sure, ask your teenager [s] how they would explain what God is like to someone who didn't know Him. How has your life affected your teenagers' idea of God? [That's a question to think about, not answer here.

3. What attribute of God would you like to model better in the next few months?

PARENTING—CALLED TO CHANGE

How can we change? Well first we need to be convinced that we can change and that we want to change. Do you really want to be less of a perfectionist or a legalist, more of a Godly model or more consistent? Whichever change you want, work through it step-by-step using the "Behavior or Attitude Change Plan'' in this ''What is Your Plan'' section.

WHAT IS YOUR PLAN?

1. **Look back through the chapter and decide which kind of parent you would like to become more of. eg. accepting, trustworthy, Godly etc. Pick one.**

2. **Which kind of parent would you like to become less of? eg. legalistic, stingy etc. Pick one.**

3. **Begin to think of at least three ways you could change to be more like what you want and less like what you don't want. What can you <u>do</u>?**

   a. _____

   _____

   b. _____

   _____

   c. _____

   _____

4. What is the cost in time, effort, money etc. of changing?

5. How will you maintain this new attitude or behavior?

6. How will you celebrate your goal?

FOOTNOTES

1. These role extremes are based on research by Coleman (1964) and adapted from a book for teenagers by Thomas D. Gragey called **How To Put Up With Parents.**

CHAPTER III

How to Trust Your Teenager

"I won't, I promise I won't."

You've heard those words before, and somehow they don't reassure you very much. Right now you would like some assurance, some indication that she is really telling the truth. You used to be able to tell by the expression on her face when she meant what she was saying, but she's grown more subtle since those days. And the problems then were so much simpler. This morning your wife found some marijuana in Lisa's room and you've been dreading this confrontation since the minute she called.

"How do I know you won't?"

You keep telling yourself that it's just marijuana; that some of your friend's kids were into it at a much younger age, that she still talks with you, that things could be worse. It's not as if she is hooked or dealing (addicted or peddling it). Or is she?

"You'll have to trust me."

Maybe she's been smoking the stuff for a long time now—away from home and only recently been bold enough to bring it into the house. Maybe she's into other things, too; like pills or sex with her boyfriend. But wouldn't there have been a hint before now if she were? How can you make this the end and not the beginning?

"I wish I could trust you when you say you won't."

But the stakes are too high. She's into stuff that could ruin her life! And look at the effect she might have on her little brothers; they are so vulnerable right now. And what about the kids at church—they must be getting a kick out of watching Lisa get away with murder.

"Why can't you?"

"Lisa, honey, you know I haven't been able to trust you for at least three years now. We've caught you lying repeatedly, you never keep your promises, you don't do your work around the house, you've embarrassed us many times with your language around our friends, and you don't even look your mother or me in the eye anymore!"

TO TRUST OR NOT TO TRUST?

Lisa's parents are struggling with a problem that most parents of teenagers face with at least one of their teenagers. The problem may be marijuana, sex, the car, friends, declining grades, or any of a hundred other items, but the one basic issue is trust-worthiness.

One reason many parents find it difficult to trust their teenagers is that their teenagers have taught them not to trust. They have done this either by being erratic with assignments and requests their parents give them or by consistently thwarting their parents' wishes with the goal of frustrating them. In most cases, being erratic started well before adolescence. Once it is habitual, it is a difficult pattern to change. Having an erratic teenager is frustrating because being erratic is a form of passive resistance.

Some parents find it difficult to trust their teenagers because they don't have much trust to invest in anybody. Trust is an investment, not a purchase. It's an investment of time, energy, and resources that may be lost if the "trustee" is not reliable. Really, it's an investment of faith in the character of another person. Some parents are very conservative with their trust investments. They are like the banker who wants a lot of collateral and a good credit rating before he will loan any money. These parents won't trust their teenager unless he has built up a history of reliability or unless they know that he has too much to lose if he doesn't come through. They don't give their children much chance to practice reliability when they are young. When these children become teenagers it's even harder to start trusting them.

In contrast, many parents are more liberal with their trust investments. Sometimes they overinvest and get burned, but they cope with their embarrassment and continue trusting.

Another reason some parents find it difficult to trust their teenagers is that they don't trust themselves. This is the parent whose security is in his identification with his job or station in life. As long as he is part of "the organization," he's secure. (A mother's "organization" may be her family.) This parent usually has a lot of investment in the status quo and sees his teenager as innocent but about to be seduced by modern society. So any rejection of accepted ideas or norms by the teenager is rejection of "the right way" to live, and therefore quite threatening.

The opposite of the parent who cannot trust himself is the parent who can trust nobody but himself. This parent has coped successfully with life's prob-

lems and admires others who also have been successful. But this parent has too much invested in his teenagers to allow them to be unsuccessful. So he has to
keep coaching his teenagers and covering for them
when they make a mistake. Mistakes are costly in
time, energy and money, so he cannot allow mistakes and consequently cannot trust his teenager.

Somewhere between the parent who cannot trust
himself and the parent who trusts no one but himself is the parent who is self-confident enough to be
able to trust other people, including his teenagers.
He knows there are times when his teenagers will
take advantage of him, but that is not such a threatening prospect that he loses his ability to trust them.

WHAT DO YOU THINK?

1. **On a scale of 1-10, ten being high trust, how much
   do you trust your teenagers?** _____
2. **On the same scale what score would your
   teenagers give you?** _____
3. **What would be the cost to you of trusting your
   teenagers with each of the following items?**
   Their own phone _____
   Their own car _____
   Their own checking account _____
   A joint checking account with you _____
   A summer-long trip across the continent _____
   No time limits on dates _____
   **Care of the house while you're on
   vacation** _____

GREAT IS HIS FAITHFULNESS

In chapter one we saw how God's faithfulness is

demonstrated by the father of the prodigal son in Luke 15. Let's look at god's faithfulness a little closer.

Faithfulness, said another way is "being full of faith." What is faith? Hebrews 11:1 gives the classic definition of faith. In many instances in Scripture faith and trust are interchangeable words. Faith in Christ is trust that He is God and that He will keep His promise to us. Establishing a personal relationship with God is simply trusting God.

The person who is getting to know God experiences His trustworthiness. God does not disappoint us. I Corinthians 1:9 and 10:13 speak of His faithfulness, as do many other passages. When Scripture speaks of God's faithfulness it is speaking about God's reliability.

LIVING TRUST

The starting point in trusting your teenager is trust or faith in God for three reasons. First, a parent can bank on God's reliability in his own life and so he can trust God to be working in the life of his teenager as well. God does hear the prayer of His children so when we pray we can trust Him to work in the lives of our teenagers even if they are resisting Him.

Second, as a parent learns to trust God more and more in greater and more intimate areas of his life, he learns how to trust people, including his teenagers. When his teenager is unreliable, God is still reliable so a parent who is trusting God is better able to handle his teenager's unreliability than a parent who has no one to trust.

Third, a parent's trust in God can be a model for his teenager to follow. The clearest picture of active faith in God that a teenager will be able to see is his parents trusting God in regards to him. In other words, because God is reliable, we parents are called to trust Him in front of our teenagers so they can understand God better by watching us.

Not only is God trustworthy, reliable, and faithful, He also invests in us, His children. Here, again, we learn how to be better parents by watching and copying God's relationship with His children. God's greatest investment was to send His only Son, Jesus, to die on a cross for us so that we might have life through Him. God made Jesus "who knew no sin to be sin on our behalf, that we might become the righteousness of God in Him" (2 Corinthians 5:21). God invests in us, His children today, working in us "both to will and to work for His good pleasure" (Philippians 2:13).

God continues to invest His riches, His reputation, His love in us even when we mismanage His trust repeatedly. In fact, let's face it, what businessman would continue to invest in a venture that yielded such low returns as God's investments in us yield?

As parents of teenagers we experience times when the returns on our investments of trust are low. It's at these times that we are most tempted not to trust any more. Our own security needs are highest and we're probably feeling foolish for having trusted our teenager in the first place. It's at these times when we most need to trust God, then invest more trust in our teenagers. By doing so, we demonstrate living trust.

It is when God's children are the most unreliable that God assures us of His faithfulness. When we're in the middle of temptation, God is faithful (1

Corinthians 10:13). When we are vacillating, God is faithful (2 Corinthians 1:17-18). Paul writes Timothy a "trustworthy statement" in 2 Timothy 2:11-13 that shows the extent of God's faithfulness.

"For if we died with Him, we shall also live with Him;

If we endure, we shall also reign with Him;

If we deny Him, He also will deny us;

If we are faithless, He remains faithful;

for He cannot deny Himself."

Following the progression in these verses, we would expect to read "If we are faithless, He drops His faith in us," But no, it's when we are most unreliable that God is still faithful!

WHAT DO YOU THINK?

1. **What is one way you might invest trust in your teenager [s] that you've not attempted yet?**

FORGIVING: THE KEY TO YOUR TRUST

How can God continue to trust us when we have repeatedly trespassed and disobeyed Him? The answer is that He has truly forgiven us. Jesus' death on the cross allowed God to extend complete forgiveness to all who accept it. Colossians 2:13-14 shows some of what is involved when God forgives. "And when you were dead in your transgressions and the uncircumcision of your flesh, He made you alive together with Him, having forgiven us all our transgressions, having cancelled out the certificate of debt consisting of decrees against us and which was hostile to us; and He has taken it out of the way, having nailed it to the cross."

Can we learn to forgive the way God forgives? Not only can we, but Ephesians 4:32 says "And be kind to one another, tenderhearted, forgiving each other, **just as** God in Christ also has forgiven you." Putting Colossians 2:13-14 and Ephesians 4:32 together, we can determine some of the elements of forgiving— the key to trusting.

Nail the transgressions to the cross. When a teenager disobeys, embarrasses or goes contrary to his parents' wishes, there's a natural feeling we all get that we've been "ripped off." If someone as close to us as our teenager doesn't respect us enough to obey, how can we respect ourselves? The natural tendency is to get even or to seek revenge. It stems from a feeling of being hurt which is usually replaced by anger. The anger is protective. It allows us to keep our self-respect by focusing on the other person, in this case our teenager.

If we express our anger immediately and punish our teenager we tend to feel better. Our self-respect is restored and our hurt stings less, particularly if the punishment in some way equals the crime. We have "gotten even" again. The problem is we may have overreacted, punished without knowing all the facts and therefore punished unjustly, or provoked our teenagers to more anger. More accurately the problem is that we have punished instead of disciplining. If we parents are "disciplining" to get even or to express our anger and frustration, we are not "disciplining," we're punishing.

God disciplines His children. The difference between His discipline and His punishment is obvious if we compare Hebrews 12:5-7 and Romans

1:18 - 2:11. God punishes in wrath, He disciplines in love.

But notice, when God nailed the "certificate of decrees against us" to the cross, Jesus took all God's punishment on Himself. So God doesn't have to punish His children!

Jesus died for our teenagers' transgressions too. So we can simply pray "Father, you sent Jesus to die for our sins, both mine and my son's (or daughter's). I don't want to hold this disobedience against my teenager and I don't really need to get even. The price of forgiveness has already been paid by Jesus on the cross so I can forgive. Now help me find the appropriate discipline to apply in this situation, I pray, in Jesus' name, Amen."

We deal with our anger, our desire for revenge, our need for self-respect before we deal with our teenager and the problem at hand. This way we can discipline instead of punish.

Cancel the debts. There are times in every parent's life when he lets his teenagers get away with "minor offenses," and sometimes even major ones. Sometimes he doesn't find out about them until a month, six months, a year or more later. The problem doesn't loom large, so he doesn't make a big deal out of it. Other times the problem is more immediate, but the parent is in a good mood, and doesn't want to take the time and emotional energy to deal with it. Sometimes parents let things go because they fear their teenagers' reactions if they make an issue of the problem.

When a lot of little problems go unresolved, they tend to accumulate. Parents don't think about them until a big problem comes along, then we use them as ammunition to prove our point. They may prove our point, but they may do more damage than good because by using them we are usually attacking our teenager's character rather than dealing with the issue at hand.

Forgiving, just as God in Christ has forgiven us, means cancelling the debts. It means resisting the impulse to bring them up as Lisa's dad brought up three years of being unable to trust her in the illustration at the beginning of this chapter. It may mean asking our teenager's forgiveness if we brought up old problems inpulsively, in the heat of an argument.

Cancelling is a continuous process for us if we are going to avoid punishing. Cancelling debts is one way to keep our focus on the future, thereby disciplining instead of punishing.

WHAT DO YOU THINK?

1. **When your spouse says "She's done it again," what is "it"?**

2. **What do you fear most that your teenager is liable to do?**

   Has your teenager done this before? Are you expecting him or her to do it again? _____

3. **Does your teenager seem to have a "bad attitude"?**
   These are signals that some of the debts may not

have been cancelled. To work through cancelling debts see the ''What Is Your Plan'' section at the end of this chapter.

Be kind. Webster's dictionary defines ''kind'' as sympathetic, gentle, benevolent. Not only does Ephesians 4:32 tie forgiving to kindness, but so does Psalm 86:5 which says ''For Thou, Lord are good, and ready to forgive, and abundant in loving-kindness to all who call upon thee.'' Forgiveness springs much easier from an attitude of kindness than from an attitude of defensiveness.

When we feel threatened, we naturally get defensive. Replacing defensiveness with kindness means we become vulnerable to being taken advantage of again. That's why being kind is sometimes very difficult. It takes generosity and an ability to sympathize with our teenager. It takes an ability to be gentle rather than tough. It takes a strong person to be gentle, and sometimes we don't feel strong. But we are called by Scripture to be kind, so we are promised strength as well. Psalm 28:7 says, ''The Lord is my strength and my shield; my heart trusts in Him, and I am helped; therefore my heart exults, and with my song I shall thank Him.''

Be tenderhearted. Being kind implies some vulnerability. But being tenderhearted implies even more vulnerability. It means we can absorb some hurt so our teenagers can grow. It means letting our walls down and inviting our family to feel our emotions with us. It also means feeling their emotions with them. When we can be tenderhearted, it becomes much easier to forgive.

The opposite of tenderheartedness is hardness of heart. In Mark 10:5 Jesus says hardness of heart was the reason Moses wrote the law on divorce. In other words, tenderhearted couples don't need divorce. Tenderhearted people can forgive. The same is true of parent-teen relationships. It takes tenderhearted, forgiving parents to develop tenderhearted, forgiving teenagers.

WHAT IS YOUR PLAN?

1. Below is a list of reasons that parents give for mistrusting their teenagers, please place a 1 next to the one most likely to be your reason, a 2 next to the second most likely reason, etc. down to the least likely reason. At the bottom there is room to add a reason of your own. Do this for each teenager in your family.
   a. Our teenager has taught us not to trust him/her._____
   b. I don't have much trust to invest._____
   c. I don't trust myself enough to trust my teenager._____
   d. I can't trust anyone but myself._____
   e. _____
2. If you need to forgive a family member
   a. Specify what you are forgiving by writing it down.
   b. Pick a time when you are not angry or likely to get angry and tell the family member you need to forgive him or her of something, then tell him or her what it is. Whether or not the family member asked for forgiveness or even ac-

cepts it is not important as the fact that you forgive him.

c. Ask God in prayer to help you forget the infraction that you've forgiven.

d. Burn the paper on which you wrote the infraction or list of infractions.

e. If you recall the infraction again, concentrate instead on reasons you are thankful for this family member and love him or her.

CHAPTER IV

Your Family Atmosphere

The family atmosphere is the thermostat for the type of communication you will have in your home. First of all, what do you mean by ''a family.'' Take a minute and write down your definition.

_____

_____

_____

Now consider this definition: ''A family is an organism that provides an atmosphere of support, encouragement, and positive opportunities for growth, which include enabling each person to come to a knowledge, understanding, and acceptance of God and Jesus Christ and a knowledge, understanding, and acceptance of himself (acquiring a positive concept).

This is an ideal, or a goal, and it **is** attainable. You as family members are very involved with one another and you effect one another whether you realize it or not. Each of you has the choice of providing positive or negative input to the other members.

Parents, however, create and stabilize the family atmosphere. The teenager should not have to set the tone for the family. Many parents say, "If only my son or daughter were different or would do what he should, we could be happy and satisfied again." The Scriptures do not teach that happiness or joy is conditioned upon the proper behavior of all family members. The teaching of James 1:2, 3 can be applied to the family situation. "Consider it wholly joyful, my brethren, whenever you are enveloped in or encounter trials of any sort, or fall into various temptations. Be assured and understand that the trial and proving of your faith bring out endurance and steadfastness and patience" (AMP). A parent's happiness or optimistic outlook does not have to be bound into the frequent mood swings of his adolescent. No one is saying that maintaining your stability in the midst of turmoil is easy, but it is possible.

The definition of "family" stresses the importance of the atmosphere being such that **each person's** self-concept can grow and develop as it should. Unfortunately, the atmosphere of many Christian homes are just the opposite. This other kind of atmosphere has been called a "depressogenic environment," for it can actually cause depression. Here it is used as a model of what a family atmosphere should not be like as the parent-teen relationship is considered.

Let's look at several specific characteristics of this environment.

DISALLOWING INDEPENDENCE

A depressogenic or negative atmosphere keeps an individual from finding some degree of independence while one or several members of the family maintain control. If a teenager needs anything, it is the opportunity to become a self-sustaining, independent person able to make mature decisions for himself according to his own set of internalized values. But some parents do not want to let go and let grow because the young person might make the wrong decision or mar their reputation. Sometimes it is just quicker and easier for parents to "do it themselves." But individuals only grow or learn when they have the freedom to try and fail and then try again and succeed according to their ability.

How can parents encourage responsible independence in their young persons? They should have begun this process in the child's preschool years. But if parents did not implement some of the principles, there is still time to do so at this point.

First, a teenager needs to know what is expected of him. He needs to know the limits for his behavior and the consequences for not staying within those limits. If a teenager is expected home at 12:00, he needs to know that 12:01 is late just as 12:30 is late and that the consequences will be enforced in both cases. If the rule has been established in advance that a violation of the curfew means losing driving privileges, and this has been written into the dating or driving covenant, very little need be said concerning the consequences. This is not a rigid approach but a responsible one. (If an emergency does occur for which the teenager is not responsible and the parents are phoned prior to the time, naturally an attitude of grace should be employed.)

As a teenager grows, it is important that a parent work with him to assist him in developing his own inner set of morals and standards. Far too many teenagers come from Christian homes in which they give verbal assent to their parents' or church's values. But when they are out of the jurisdiction or away from the influence of home or church, they become very unstable when confronted with other value systems.

An ineffective approach to insuring moral values in a teenager is the **overreaction technique**—a constant, critical, negative attack upon non-Christian standards or behavior. Whenever a belief or behavior appears in a magazine, newspaper or on TV, dogmatic and belittling comments are made in the presence of the child so he will see the wrongness of the object being attacked.

Too often, however, this approach can have just the opposite effect. Some teenagers simply tune out the overreacting parent and wait until he is away from home to pursue this different lifestyle. They nod assent when in the presence of their parents, but as soon as the opportunity presents itself, their behavior begins to reflect what their parents have been preaching against.

A positive method of attempting to build values in the life of a teenager is the **inoculation approach**. Sometimes when a person is given a shot from a medical doctor to gain immunity against a disease, he is given a small dosage of that disease which enables him to resist it should he later come into direct contact with it. The same principle can be applied in the teaching of values to children.

As a child develops through the preschool and primary years, he is learning the parents' value system through example and open discussion. Upon reaching the junior age (9 to 11) a child is old enough to begin this discussion process with his parents. Here the parents seek to engage their children in a discussion of opposing viewpoints. They talk with (not to) the child or teenager about different value systems and they discuss the pros and cons and consequences of each. They give him small doses of these various points of view so when the child comes face to face with them he is aware of what they are and prepared to deal with them. He is also aware of why he believes as he does and why it is of value to him.

Often these discussions are carried on using a case study approach where different value systems can be applied to the problem being presented. Especially in the area of dating and sexual behavior, a teenager needs to know what and why he believes. He needs to have formulated ideas of how to maintain his standard well in advance of situations in which someone else challenges his beliefs. If you have not done this in your home yet, why not begin to initiate these discussions?

Another method of assisting a teenager develop responsible independence is to get him started in the process of earning money and paying for some of his items. Too many youths have been given so much that they have failed to grasp the reality of the hard work involved in paying for material goods. They observe parents paying for most of their items with a credit card and develop their own philosophy of life upon this kind of economic system. Constant credit card buying does not teach the inner discipline of delaying rewards of satisfaction of desires until a person has the means in hand to purchase the goods. This attitude may be generalized and transferred to other areas of life such as the pursuit of education for a better vocational choice or sexual behavior.

ENCOURAGING DEPENDENCE

Another characteristic of an environment that hampers the self-concept development of a person is a home that encourages dependence. When a child or teenager is convinced that he cannot possibly survive without the emotional support of another member of the household, he becomes over-dependent. This makes him feel that he cannot make proper decisions without his parents' involvement or constantly checking up on him.

Some parents have a difficult time when their teenager is away at camp or on an outing. They call each day and check up on their teenager, creating this dependent relationship, and in many cases embarrassing the teenager.

PROVOKING GUILT

Still another symptom of the depressogenic atmosphere is the repeated provoking of guilt regardless of the facts. Statements to a teenager that convey the message that he is responsible for the disruption of the family, the mother's depression and worry, the poor communication, or the other children's discouragement do not help him. How does this characteristic relate to Colossians 3:21?

SUPPRESSING EMOTIONS

Another depressing characteristic in some families

is a refusal to permit any show of emotion and, in particular, healthy reactions to anger. The denial of our emotional life has very serious consequences for us psychologically and physiologically. Emotions are a gift from God. He created us with the capacity to experience them.

Teenagers need a healthy model of emotional expression from their parents. Open discussions of emotions and ways of expressing feelings can be very beneficial for the teenager. Seeing a parent openly talk about why they become angry and how they are learning to release that anger in a healthy manner is a good model for the teenager. Seeing the parents practice Ephesians 4:26 is beneficial.

It is very important for every member of a family to understand the causes of depression and how to help one another when this occurs. (See **An Answer to Depression** by Norman Wright, Harvest House Publishers.) Perhaps we don't care for the ways our teenagers express their feelings. When family members are calm is an appropriate time to discuss proper ways of expressing themselves.

BLOCKING COMMUNICATION

A final characteristic of a depressogenic environment is the blocking of open and direct communication. We must communicate to live and to have quality relationships.

CAN I CHANGE?

Can any parent change? Some parents see their patterns of relating to their families as so much a part of their lifestyle that they feel they can't change. They have been reinforcing a habit for so long they may be comfortable with it even though it makes their family uncomfortable. It is threatening for him to change the way he relates to those closest to him—maybe they won't be able to cope with their changed spouse, dad, or mom.

Maybe that's why God is so patient with His children. He keeps hoping we'll change—be transformed as it says in Romans 12:2. He wants us to keep putting off the old naturally selfish ways of living and putting on the new ways which are led by His Spirit who lives in us.

Here is a suggested way to change. Take a 3-by-5 card and write the word "STOP" in big enough letters to cover the card. On the reverse side of the card write the words, "I want to be more . . ." and finish the sentence with the change you want to make concerning your life.

Keep the card with you for a month. Whenever you hear yourself slipping back to the old pattern, pull out the card, say "stop" out loud, read the back side of the card out loud, and start looking for an alternative to the old pattern. You may have to postpone making a decision for 5 to 10 minutes while you come up with an alternative.

WHAT'S YOUR PLAN?
BEHAVIOR OR ATTITUDE CHANGE PLAN SHEET

1. **Describe the behavior or attitude that you want to change.**

2. List several very important reasons for giving up and/or changing this behavior.

3. Motivation to change is very important. From your reasons listed in #2, select the most important reason. Write it down.

4. Begin to think about how you should change your behavior or attitude. List some possible ways.

5. a. What has been your attitude toward changing this behavior or attitude in the past? Describe.

   b. Indicate what attitude you are going to have now.

   c. How will you maintain this new attitude? List at least three ways.

6. Whenever you eliminate a behavior or attitude that you dislike often a vacuum or void will

remain. Frequently a person prefers the bad or poor behavior to this emptiness so he reverts back to the previous pattern. In order for this not to happen substitute a POSITIVE BEHAVIOR in place of the negative. Describe what you can substitute for the behavior or attitude that you are giving up.

7. Can you think of any scriptures that would apply to this problem area. List the positive behavior or attitude that these Scriptures suggest in place of the negative. Write out the way you see yourself putting this Scripture into action in your life. Describe the consequences of thinking or behaving in this new way.

FOOTNOTE

Material in this chapter has been adapted from **How to Put up with Parents: A Guide for Teenagers** by Thomas D. Gnagey (Ottawa, Ill.: Facilitation House, 1975), and from **An Answer to Parent-Teen Relationships** by Norman Wright (Irvine, Calif.: Harvest House Publishers, 1977).

CHAPTER V

Troublesome Teens

"But you don't understand our problem," commented the father with a smile. "We've followed your principles. We've read all the books, listened to all the tapes we could find, gone to seminars. We've been accepting and we've been firm. But now he's down at juvenile hall, picked up on a dope charge. We'd like to try communicating with our teenager, but he doesn't want anything to do with us."

"I've heard of wife beating and child abuse," a middle-aged lady said as tears welled up in her eyes. "But I've never heard of mother beating and I don't know what to do. My collarbone is healed now but I'm afraid of my own son."

"Our son took a baseball bat to our living room," said another dad. "I guess it's a good thing I wasn't home or one of us might have gotten badly hurt. Most of the time he's an O.K. kid. But when he gets angry he's liable to do anything."

"We don't think of ourselves as terrible parents said another well-dressed businessman. We have two kids in college and a high schooler who loves us. They have always been obedient and quite civilized. Our home is a happy place, except for our junior higher. We just can't cope with him, and nothing works. He's a different species from the rest of our kids."

Maybe you can identify with these parents. One or more of your teenagers has to "do his own thing," and any attempt to build communication with him is greeted with derision. He deliberately disobeys, lies all the time, and seems to try his best to be everything you disapprove of. The suggestion that you try again to rebuild bridges to your teenager fills you with dread or pain, or maybe even a sense of futility. You've tried repeatedly in the past only to be disappointed. And maybe your struggle has had harmful side effects on the rest of your family.

Before responding to the suggestion that you try again to rebuild bridges, you might consider some questions together as a couple. Write your answers individually first, then compare notes and discuss.

WHAT DO YOU THINK?

1. **What do you love about your teenager? List all the things you can think of.**

2. **How do you love your teenager? Indicate how your love is expressed.**

3. **How might you express your love in some alternate ways?**

4. When do you express your love to your teenager? Do you express love on your own initiative or only in response to something your teenager says or does?

OPTIONS

Is there one right way to handle a kid who is causing serious disturbances in your family? Probably not, or you would have found it yourself some time ago. So let's start by considering the options, including those you may have tried. At one extreme you could kill your teenager. We mention this option tongue-in-cheek only to suggest one extreme. At the other extreme you could do nothing. If you go about denying that there is really a problem, maybe it will go away. We mention this option tongue-in-cheek only because it is one so commonly taken and it represents the other extreme. Doing nothing prolongs both your problems and your teenager's problems.

WHAT DO YOU THINK?

1. Let's start by listing all the options you've already tried.

2. Between the two extremes what other options can you think of? At this point think together as parents and jot down ideas. Don't evaluate or judge the ideas, just get them down on paper.

Now let's evaluate each option. A key question to ask about each idea you listed is whether it is a way of disciplining or a way of punishing your teenager. Dr. Bruce Narramore in his book, **Help! I'm A Parent** makes the distinction between punishment and discipline quite explicit. The following chart is taken from his book.

PUNISHMENT AND DISCIPLINE

	PUNISHMENT	DISCIPLINE
PURPOSE	To inflict penalty for an offense	To train for correction and maturity
FOCUS	Past misdeeds	Future correct deeds
ATTITUDE	Hostility and frustration on the part of the parent	Love and concern on the part of the parent
RESULTING EMOTION IN THE CHILD	Fear and guilt	Security

As Dr. Narramore shows, God doesn't punish His children, He disciplines us. His punishment is reserved for people who never accept Jesus' death on the cross as payment of the penalty for their sins. God's discipline of His children can be a model for us to follow when disciplining our children.

WHAT DO YOU THINK?

1. **Try applying Dr. Narramore's chart to each option you come up with, and cross out each one that is a way to punish rather than discipline.**

2. **How many ideas are left? If you had to cross out most of your ideas you may want to get a copy of Dr. Narramore's book for more detailed input on discipline and punishment.**

INVESTING IN FUTURES

Several years ago a friend of ours was investing in the commodities market. We met him at a broker's office several mornings at 7:00 and watched the price quotes as they changed. Our friend was investing in the future price of corn. At the time it was Spring and he figured that the price of corn in July would be considerably lower than what everybody else figured it would be. So he gave $1,000 to his broker who entered it for him, and we watched the price of corn go up every day until one day it plunged and our friend made something like $875 profit on his investment.

Maybe we can borrow some ideas from our friend and translate them into the business of relationships with teenagers. If so, the first parallel is that raising teenagers, like playing the commodities market is a risky business. In other markets there are guarantees to help keep a person from losing his investment. In commodities a person can lose his investment quickly—it's risky. There are few guarantees in the business of raising teenagers. In this chapter we're concentrating on teenagers who are

already in serious trouble—an even riskier investment than the average teenager. But change—any
change—requires investment.

WHAT DO YOU THINK?

1. **Since change requires investment, what are you
   willing to invest in your teenager? Here are some
   ideas to start you thinking:**
   a. **A complete vacation where you do whatever
      your teenager wants you to do with him or her.**
   b. **Sacrificing your overtime with its extra income
      so you can spend some evenings and week-
      ends with your teenager.**
   c. **The price of an airline ticket or other expenses
      for your teenager's best friend so he can
      accompany you on your vacation.**
   d. **Sacrificing some of your nights out with your
      friends to sit around and rap with your teen-
      ager.**
   e. **A weekly family night home where you think,
      talk, and plan together.**
   f. **Transferring some of your power as a parent
      to your teenager as an investment in his de-
      cision-making ability. For example, let your
      teenager choose your next car.**

If investment is so risky, why do **you** have to do all
the investing? You don't. First of all, remember that
God has already invested the life and blood of His
only Son, Jesus, in your teenager. He made that
investment whether your teenager ultimately responds or not. Secondly, you can help your teenager

to change by eliciting his investment in change. How can you do this?

Communicate until you get your teenager to make a value statement. See if you can find out what he prizes. You may have a pretty good idea already, but take the time to test your ideas of your teenager's values against what he says he values. Often there's a difference between what a teenager values and what his parents think he values. Parents may have accepted stereotypes about young people that don't fit their teenager. A teenager may have changed values wihout communicating the change to his folks.

Often the real value lies behind rather than within the behavior the parents object to. For instance parents may believe their teenager prizes alcohol, whereas their teenager may not value the alcohol so much as the feelings he gets of being powerful when he's drinking.

It's not enough to find out one value. Keep communicating—asking questions and sharing your own values. Avoid two things, though: 1) trying to convince your teenager of the superiority of your values or the inferiority of his; and 2) asking why questions about your teenager's values. Over time, as you discover your teenager's values, write them down so you won't forget them.

Tie the achievement of something your teenager values to a behavior you value. For instance, let's say your teenager's highest value, and seemingly his only value is getting stoned on dope. Let's also assume you are totally against dope. But no matter what you've done, your teenager still chooses and values getting stoned. You aren't going to have to condone his getting stoned. Since you know that getting dope costs money, make his allowance (if you're still giving him one) or your signature on his driver's license contingent upon his working with you three consective Saturdays and taking a weekend camping trip together on the fourth Saturday. All this time he must stay clean (no dope). Let him know that if he accomplishes these objectives you will give him the reward you promise and he may spend it or use it as he wishes; you won't hassle him about that.

If your teenager laughs off the idea, you have two options. You can increase the stakes making the reward a stronger motivator, or you can restrict the rewards he's already getting for his present behavior. A third option is to do both. Examples of increasing the stakes would be increasing an allowance giving him a one-time bonus of money, or purchase of a much-desired part for his stereo, etc. Examples of restricting the rewards would be witholding your teenager's allowance, restricting his use of the car or taking away his driver's license, in other words making him more dependent on you. Remember, you're not doing this to punish him for past misbehavior but to help him learn better uses of his money, time and energies.

If he agrees to your proposal, stick to your plan. The idea of working together for three Saturdays and camping on the fourth Saturday is just an example of some behaviors you might want to suggest. We chose it as an example because it has some implicit benefits. One is the benefit of being together every weekend. It gives you a chance to listen to your teenager and answer his questions. Being together by plan for a long enough time period allows for the possibility of communication—the key to your teen-ager.

Another benefit is that the value you place in being with your teenager is communicated nonverbally in a powerful way. If you value him enough to give up other pursuits (like your business) to be with him, you let him know he's valuable as a person in your eyes.

Once you've agreed upon a goal, help your teen-ager make a plan for achieving it. At first the goals need to be small enough steps that they are fairly readily achievable. Then, as your teenager achieves the first goals, set new goals that are a little more ambitious. Help your teenager make his own plans for achieving these goals. The self-respect he will gain, first by achieving some easier goals, then by making plans and carrying them out to the achieve-ment of more ambitious goals, will allow your teen-ager to choose new values.

Discourage isolation, and encourage relationships that will help your teenager. This doesn't mean that you won't allow him ever to see his loaded buddies again, nor does it mean you're constantly setting him up with ''nice church kids.'' Your teenager chooses friends to compliment his own identity at the time. As he adds new values he'll begin looking for peers that share his new values. But you can discourage holding on to old friends who complement and rein-force his old behavior patterns. He may hold on to old friends much longer than he needs them, probably because he's not made the new friends he needs. Be patient, and try to expose him to many other teen-agers, not just a few you approve of.

Help your teenager choose new goals. Once he is

used to making plans for achieving your shared goals, encourage him to begin choosing goals he wants to reach. This will probably start by his suggestions of alternatives to a goal you've picked. Encourage this kind of planning for it helps a teenager become more goal oriented. Make sure the goals are reachable, measureable, and that you both can own the goals. Also make sure they are limited in terms of time.

At this point you may want to suggest involvement in Scripture together as one of your together goals. You might both read a book like Ephesians or Colossians and then discuss it together. Involvement in Scripture is more likely to be accepted and profitable than involvement in church. If your teenager doesn't want involvement in Scripture, don't force it. Remember, it's the Holy Spirit who draws people to God.

From the beginning, it's important to seek commitment. If you've suggested a series of Saturdays or some other behavior, don't start until your teenager has made a commitment to you verbally that he wants to invest in your suggestion. Postpone starting until you have the commitment. Don't assume anything. Be very specific about what you expect and what your teenager can expect.

Then once your teenager has committed himself to a specific behavior, accept no excuses for violations. If your teenager can get away with excuses it will lower his respect for you and his respect for himself. So if he blows it, and he will, start over—make a new goal and plan.

WHAT IS YOUR PLAN?

1. **To get you started, try writing your teenager's five highest values here.**

   1. _____

   2. _____

   3. _____

   4. _____

   5. _____

2. **Now communicate with your teenager. Take time to restate more accurately each value, or put in new ones, then reprioritize them once you've listed them all.**

   Priority #

   1. _____   _____

   2. _____   _____

   3. _____   _____

   4. _____   _____

   5. _____   _____

FOOTNOTE

1. Dr. Bruce Narramore, **Help! I'm a Parent** (Grand Rapids, Mi.: Zondervan Publishing House, 1972), p. 41.

CHAPTER VI

Their Friends and Yours

Can you picture your teens' friends? Can you see their faces in your mind? Close your eyes for a minute and flash images of them on the inside of your eyelids.

Maybe you saw the neighbor's teenager who's been your son's friend since they met in the fourth grade. He's been in your house almost as much as in his own.

Maybe you saw your daughter's slumber party; mess all over the house, but talk and laughter most of the night.

Maybe you saw his high school church group or her friend from "Pioneer girls" days. Or maybe you saw his girlfriend—her picture on his dresser.

Maybe you saw her boyfriend—the one whose lifestyle seems to be so opposite yours. You're hoping it won't get too serious.

What a mural they make! Blue jeans, T-shirts with every kind of message, tennis shoes, sandals, dresses of varying lengths, long hair, "perms," color-coordinated outfits, period costumes, beards, pimples, and football helmets all add to the color and texture of a picture that is sometimes happy, sometimes despondent, but always changing. And they are your teenagers' friends.

Wouldn't you like to choose your teenagers' friends for them? Think of the heartache it would save them as well as you. But obviously, you can't.

Which of your teenagers' friends do you like? What do you like about them? Which of your teenagers' friends threaten you or cause you anxiety? What is it that you don't particularly care for?

WHAT DO YOU THINK?

1. **If your son or daughter were answering the same questions about your friends:**
   a. **Which of your friends would he or she like?**

   b. **Which of your friends threaten him or her?**

   c. **Which of your friends do your teens not care for?**

INVEST IN YOUR TEENAGERS' FRIENDS

Maybe you're not interested in your teenagers' friends. After all, that's their business. They are strong enough to not be overly influenced by their friends. You trust them to do what's right for themselves.

Let's hope you're not in for a big surprise. Beyond that, let's hope that your trust in your teenager is warranted. But whether or not it is, you have several advantages to gain if you invest in your teenagers' friends.

You assert your love. By taking time, energy and interest in your teens' friends, you say ''I love you'' to your teen. He expects you to invest in him. Investing in his friends is an unexpected bonus. When they respond positively, your teens' love for you is enhanced.

You affirm your trust. In effect you say, "Any friend of yours is a friend of mine. I trust you to choose wisely." Your trust is likely to be reciprocated.

You enhance your teenagers' self-image. By believing in him and making that belief obvious to his friends, you enhance his belief in himself. He can then exert a stronger influence on his friends.

You build a climate of inclusion. By investing in your teens' friends, even some whom you find unattractive, you make it easy for your teen to include you rather than exclude you from his decisions. He feels that you haven't pitted yourself against his friends making him choose between you and them.

You have a positive influence. You make it easier for your teen to lead his friends to Christ. They can see the relationship you have with your teenager. If they are drawn in they will be affected by your values. They may not change their present course, but they will at least have to deal with the alternatives you represent.

I remember as a teenager dating a girl whose mother did not appreciate many of my values. But she included me in many of the family functions and invested a lot of time and conversation in me. Her husband took a personal interest in me too. This couple's influence on me was much longer lasting than the dating relationship I had with their daughter.

THE BIBLE ON FRIENDS

The Bible has much to say about friendships. The nature of God's relationship to His people and how we can enjoy that relationship is central to the whole Biblical message.

The book of Proverbs deals with friendship and the choice of friends specifically. Some aspects of friendship it deals with are:

1. Determining what kind of friends your friends are—Proverbs 9:7-9, 10:8-11, 17:4-5, 17:17, 19:22, 20:11.

2. Choosing friends carefully—Proverbs 13:20, 20:6-7, 27:17, 28:7, 29:24.

3. Avoiding some "friends"—Proverbs 14:7, 18:24, 20:19, 22:24-25, 23:20-21, 29:3.

WHAT DO YOU THINK?

1. **Is your choice of friends a model you want your teens to follow?**

2. **Are you a friend to your teen or just a parent? What do you do to enhance your friendship with your teens?**

3. **Are you a friend to your teens' friends?**

YOUR TEENAGERS AND THEIR FRIENDS

The friends your teens choose will not only have an

impact on them but on you and your whole family as well. That may be obvious if their friends "hang out" at your house. But it is also true even though you see very little of them or their friends.

Often parents blame their teenagers' friends for causing a breech in relationship between them and their teenagers. "They are such a bad influence on my Jimmy," is a typical mother's complaint. She may have a valid complaint, but maybe it can be remedied.

JIM, HIS DAD, AND LARRY

Jim and his dad have had a fairly strong and stable relationship over the years. Jim has changed a lot as he grew, and so has his relationship with his dad. But it has remained positive and significant to Jim.

In high school, Jim makes a lot of new friends, one of which is Larry. At first, Jim's dad accepts Larry as he has most of Jim's friends. But soon he begins to feel that Larry is a bad influence on his son, so he finds ways to keep them apart. Jim and Larry resent this, of course, so the pressure builds.

Jim feels pressure from Larry to invest less time at home. He also feels pressure from his Dad to invest less time with Larry and more in his home and family. Larry even feels some of the pressure.

Jim's dad feels the pressure of a dilemma. If he says nothing and lets Larry keep influencing Jim he fears Jim will absorb many of Larry's attitudes and values and will alienate himself from his family. On the other hand if he fights Jim's friendship with Larry, he may fuel Jim's resentment and alienation. What's a dad to do?

WHAT DO YOU THINK?
1. If you were Jim's dad would you:
   a. Say nothing and hope Jim forgets Larry;
   b. Have a talk with Jim about how Larry is influencing him;
   c. Prohibit Jim from being Larry's friend;
   d. Insist that Jim give the church youth group equal time;
   e. Make time with Larry conditional on Jim's inviting Larry to church;
   f. Move to another city;
   g. None of the above, I would

2. How would your son or daughter respond to the solution you picked?

Before making too many decisions, it might help to consider the nature of friendships. Blaming Larry for changes in Jim's attitudes and values won't help Jim, his dad or Larry. The idea that a teenager rebels because of the influence of his friends is as old as Pinocchio, but it is not realistic. Friends may help a teenager express rebellion and may introduce new ways to rebel, but a teenager chooses friends that complement the attitudes and values he or she already has.

One author on friends states this principle this

way: "You are your friends in many ways. They reflect your moods and your characteristics, your weaknesses and strengths, and they very realistically indicate your needs, some of which you yourself may not be aware of. Looking at your friends individually and collectively, a pattern emerges, and that pattern can be a highly accurate barometer of your emotional state." [1]

So the first consideration for Jim's dad might be to look at Jim's friends as a fairly accurate indicator of what is going on in Jim's life.

One important reason then, for accepting your teenagers' friends, even if you don't approve of their attitudes and values is that they tell you a lot about your own teenagers. That doesn't mean you helplessly watch your teenager alienate himself from you and say nothing. It does mean that you try your best to avoid cutting any communication lines that exist between yourself and your teenager's friends. More positively, it means building bridges to your teenagers' friends if at all possible.

A second consideration is that we all want the people we choose as friends to be friends to each other as well. There is a natural tendency to be inclusive with friends of friends. "Any friend of yours is a friend of mine" expresses this. So a parent's friends are automatically expected to be their teenagers' friends as well. But a parent's friends more nearly complement that parent than his or her teenager. So it's natural for a teenager to build new friendships and it's the parent's turn to accommodate himself to his teenager's choice of friends. Taking Jim, his dad and Larry as an example again, let's diagram their relationship.

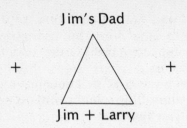

Jim's Dad

Jim + Larry

Since Jim's dad and Jim are friends, when Jim develops a friendship with Larry the natural tendency is for Jim's dad and Larry to be friendly toward each other.

But if Larry reflects some of Jim's attitudes and values that Jim's dad doesn't like, not only does he change his attitude toward Larry, but the whole "triad relationship" changes.

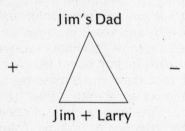

Jim's Dad

Jim + Larry

Notice the algebraic product of the signs in the diagram. If you remember your high school algebra, two pluses times a minus equals a minus. Whether you followed that or just figured it out from the description, the important thing is that this triad relationship is out of balance. There is pressure on all three persons in the triad relationship to change in some way to balance the relationship.

Jim's dad and Larry might find a way of accommodating each other, thereby, changing their negative relationship into a positive one and balancing the triad relationship.

Another way the triad relationship might become balanced again is if the relationship between Jim and his dad becomes negative.

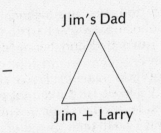

Jim's Dad

Jim + Larry

Two minuses equals a plus or a balanced triad relationship. Unfortunately this is an experience many families share. As teenagers acquire their own friends, their relationship with their parents becomes negative. In fact many parents expect this alienation and see it as a necessary part of growing up. Although the development of independence is a natural part of growing up and acquiring one's own friends is a part of this process, parent-teen alienation is not necessary.

If parents accept their teenagers and keep the channels of communication open, their teenagers are more likely in the long run to keep their relationships with their parents positive, even at the expense of some of their peer relationships. This would be the third way the triad could be balanced.

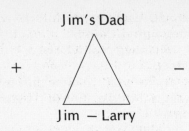

This is generally the way most parents hope that conflicts with their teenagers' friends will be resolved. But a word of caution is necessary at this point. If all parent-teen friendship conflicts are resolved this way it would indicate parental dominance and a lack of growth on the teenagers' part. The parents may also need to grow in their ability to accept or at least tolerate their teenagers' choices.

BE A FRIEND TO A FRIEND

Parents can adopt a coping strategy or they can develop a winning strategy with their teenagers' friends. A coping strategy is one that assumes conflict, loss of parent-teen relationships and alienation. "Nothing can be done about the inevitable, so just cope with it as best you can."

A winning strategy for parents is one that necessitates an investment of time, energy, and vulnerability in the attempt to win the friendship of a son or daughter's friends. A winning strategy is built on several foundations.

The first foundation is a strong positive parent-teen relationship. A relationship built on mutual trust and acceptance, an open two-way communication will be a conflict preventor.

A second foundation is to invest in your teenagers'

friends as much as possible. A word of caution is appropriate, though. Beware of trying to **control** your teenagers or their friends. You won't be helping your teenager develop self-discipline and responsibility. If you try to control your teenagers' friends, they will resent you, and withdraw, maybe taking your teenager with them.

A third foundation will be whether or not you and your teenagers have other mutual friends. If most of your teenagers' friends have positive relationships with you, it is likely that they will change their relationships with their friends rather than with you.

WHAT IS YOUR PLAN?

1. **What are some things you can do to build or rebuild your relationship with each of your teens? List them here.**

2. **Pick one of the things you listed in number one and answer the following questions. These will help you make it work.**
   a. **What aspect of your relationship do you want this action to build?**

   b. **What will you try to communicate to your teen?**

    c. Do you need to involve your spouse or anyone else? If so, who?

    d. When is a good time to try it?

3. What are some things you can do to build relationships with some of your teens' friends?

Name _____I will _____

Name _____I will _____

Name _____I will _____

4. Would your teen be open to the idea of investing together with you in some of his or her friends? How can you suggest this idea?

5. How about asking your teens to invest with you in one of your friends? Elicit his or her suggestions in finding a way to meet your friends' needs.

FOOTNOTE

1. Jerry Gilles, **Friends - The Power and Potential of the Company You Keep** (New York: Coward, McCann, & Geoghegan, 1976, p. 15).

CHAPTER VII

Different Frequencies

You are a communicator! But what do you communicate? What messages are you sending to your teenagers? Are they really getting through? Did you know that communication is one of the most frequent points of tension between teenagers and parents? In one survey parents listed lack of effective communication as the third main cause of tension between them and their teenagers. The teenagers, however, listed inability to communicate with parents as the number one cause of tension.

Where do we begin with communciation? Let's start with our thought life. What we say is simply a reflection of what we have been thinking and feeling. The parent who worries a great deal about life in general and his teenager in particular will probably convey this anxiety in most conversations with his teenager. And this could sound like overdomination, protectiveness or even lack of trust. The parent who mulls over his angry feelings is apt to reflect this in his manner of communication with his teenagers.

If our words are creating problems in our communication, let's go back to our thought life and evaluate the contents. Jesus said, "Listen, and understand this thoroughly! It is not what goes into a man's mouth that makes him unclean" (Matthew 15:10, 11 PHIL).

The transition from mind to mouth sometimes breaks down because the words we use do not correctly convey our message. Do you always mean what you say or say what you mean?

WHAT DO YOU THINK?

Try this experiment. Write down ten to fifteen of the most frequent phrases you use around the home with the family and do the same with phrases that your teenager uses. Give your teenager the list of phrases or words you use and ask him to write down what he thinks they mean. Write down what you think his phrases or words mean. Then compare!

Are you saying what you mean? Consider what James Fairfield had to say about this:

"When you speak, your meaning or intention is in your mind and only partially expressed in your words. At best, your words only sketch a picture of what you mean. At worst, what you say projects the wrong picture entirely and your meaning is lost.

"Yet we persist in believing that words in themselves hold all meaning, and all that is necessary is to look in a dictionary, check the definition listed, and we shall know exactly what the person meant who used the word. We forget that dictionaries merely collect common meanings that people give to words.

"But words do not 'mean.' Words are only conveyers of some of the meaning or intention given them by the person using them . . . When you speak to me, I can only infer what you mean; I cannot be certain unless I check my inferences with you. And this may take a little more time that we're used to giving!'' [1]

Many families complain that even though they're of the same nationality, in their home two different languages are spoken. Often they feel the need for a translator! This is true, and the reason lies in the meaning of words. Meanings are not just in words but meanings are in people too. Your meanings are inside you. Sometimes neither we nor our teenagers know what words to use to get the meaning out. Consider it in this way: [2]

If meanings are in the words:

If you have the same vocabulary, the message means the same for you and the teenager.

The listener is most responsible for the success of the communication as he has to decode the speaker's words.

If an error in communication occurs here, the problem lies with the hearer.

Feedback is not important.

Communication breakdown justifies blame.

If meanings are in the people:

Speaker and hearer will not always have exactly the same meaning for what has been said.

Here the main responsibility for the success of the communication lies with the speaker and the listener.

If an error occurs here, the main reason is because of the transaction between the two.

Feedback is important.

Communication breakdown can be altered by

| When there are differences, one person is right and one is wrong. | increased **awareness** and feedback.

There are several ways to look at the same situation and discover a solution. |

It is important that our messages are true to our meaning in order for us to be understood and for us to understand others. Too many people give bent messages or stereo messages—speaking out of both sides of their mouth at the same time. The Word of God says that we are to ''speak the truth in love'' (Ephesians 4:15).

To make sure that your message means what you want it to mean, check your tone of voice and your nonverbal behavior. These two features are better indicators of what you mean and feel than the actual words you use. If you say to your teenager that you're really interested in what went on at school on a certain day, and you say it in a flat tone of voice with your head buried behind a magazine, will he really believe you? Would you believe it? One researcher stated that the actual words we use in our face-to-face conversation makes up only 7 percent of our message while the tone of voice accounts for 38 percent and the nonverbal aspect 55 percent. [3]

If this is true, what is our tone of voice saying to the other person? If we claim that we are in control and are not angry, is our tone a giveaway? What does our body posture say to our teenager as we talk? Do we slouch, stand with hands on hips, slam the cupboard as we talk to him, cross our arms, turn our back on him, or raise our eyebrows when we say, ''And where have you been?'' All of these behaviors and actions send a message.

WHAT DO YOU THINK?

Try this experiment and discover what nonverbal messages you're sending in your home. Ask family members to write down all of the nonverbal behaviors they use in communicating with one another. Have each one write down what it means to him and then what he thinks it means to the others in the family. After each person has done this, share your results with one another. You will probably find that some behaviors are being misinterpreted, and now you can clear the air! Be sure you write this down now.

Children attending school soon learn to chant the singsong poem, ''Sticks and stones may break my bones, but words will never hurt me.'' But experience quickly teaches that this is untrue. Words can and do hurt a person. The Bible recognizes this and talks about word power in both the Old and New Testaments.

Proverbs 18:21 states what many have discovered: ''Death and life are in the power of the tongue.'' Proverbs 26:22 also speaks of how words really get to a person: ''The words of a whisperer . . . go down in the most innermost parts of the body.'' This was what Job was experiencing when he cried in frustration, ''How long will you torment me, and crush me with words?'' Or as The Living Bible puts it,

"How long are you going to trouble me, and try to break me with your words?" (Job 19:2).

James 3:2-10 talks about the power of words and why it is so important to control the tongue. Here are key ideas for improving communications:

"If anyone can control his tongue, it proves that he has perfect control over himself in every other way. We can make a large horse turn around and go wherever we want by means of a small bit in his mouth. And a tiny rudder makes a huge ship turn wherever the pilot wants it to go, even though the winds are strong.

"So also the tongue is a small thing, but what enormous damage it can do. A great forest can be set on fire by one tiny spark. And the tongue is a flame of fire. It is full of wickedness, and poisons every part of the body. And the tongue is set on fire by hell itself, and can turn our whole lives into a blazing flame of destruction and disaster.

"Men have trained, or can train, every kind of animal or bird that lives and every kind of reptile and fish, but no human being can tame the tongue. It is always ready to pour out its deadly poison. Sometimes it praises our heavenly Father, and sometimes it breaks out into curses against men who are made like God. And so blessing and cursing come pouring out of the same mouth. Dear brothers, surely this is not right!" (TLB).

James compares the power of the tongue to the rudder of a ship, as far as power is concerned. Comparatively speaking, a rudder is a small part of the ship, yet it can turn the ship in any direction and control its destiny. What husbands and wives say to one another can turn their marriage in different directions and in some cases cause them to wind up going in a vicious circle.

Continuing to emphasize the tongue's potency, James also compares it to a flame of fire. Great forests can be leveled by one tiny spark. In the same way, a family can be damaged and in some cases even "set on fire" by one remark, or (more typically) by continually chopping and chipping away at each other.

Words do spread like fire. Did you ever try to stop a rumor? Did you ever attempt to squelch an unkind story once it was told? Impossible! Who can unsay words or wipe out what has been heard?

James continues to bear down on the difficulty in controlling the tongue when he writes that man's ingenuity has succeeded in taming almost every kind of living creature; yet he has failed in taming his own tongue! According to the dictionary "to tame" means "to control" and "to render useful and bene-ficial." Man has not been able to do that with his tongue on any widespread basis.

Each person must be responsible for his own tongue-training program. Controlling the tongue needs to be a continuing aim for each husband and wife because everything that is said either helps . . or hinders; heals . . . or scars; builds up . . . or tears down. [4]

One of the main concerns I hear coming from parents is this: "Why can't my teenager act like an adult? I wish I could depend on him. I've got to get on his case again and again!" My answer doesn't entirely solve the problem but it can help. Why not treat the teenager more as an adult and show a belief in his capabilities instead of responding to him as a person younger than he actually is? But you say, "If he would act like an adult, then I would treat him like one!" Perhaps our belief and trust in a person would release him to mature faster.

Often we limit the development of an individual by our constricted view. We don't allow him enough behavioral freedom or speak to him as an adult. Often our communication pattern reflects a parent speaking to a child instead of two adults talking together. Why not respond to his potential and guide him along? First Corinthians 13 speaks of "love believing the best . . ." Could we use this to see what our teenager will develop into down the road?

In order to respond to our teenager according to his potential, several communication characteristics need to be evident in us.

WHAT'S YOUR PLAN?

If you are studying this book with your teenager, best results can be obtained if you complete the following material individually and then discuss your answers together. As you compare ideas, feelings and attitudes you will achieve new levels of communication and understanding in your family.

1. Circle the phrase that you feel describes the quality of communication in your family:
   a. needs no improvement
   b. highly effective
   c. satisfactory
   d. inconsistent
   e. superficial
   f. frustrating
   g. highly inadequate

Now go back and underline the phrases which you

think your teenager would choose.

2. List three things you can do to improve communication between yourself and your teenager. "I plan to improve our communication by:

   a. _____

   b. _____

   c. _____

   I will start doing these three things [date]_____
   _____[time_____."

3. Make an "appointment" with your teenager when you can sit down (perhaps over a cup of coffee) and plan together how you can improve your communication.
   (date)_____(time)_____
   As you do your planning together be sure to cover the four following points:

   a. Share and discuss your responses to question 1 on the quality of communication in your family.

   b. Also share your responses to question 2 on how you plan to improve communication. Ask your teenager's opinion to see if he or she feels your suggestion will actually improve communication. If not, work out alternate ideas that both of you approve of.

   c. Commit yourself to following your plans for improving communication and stick to it for at least one week.

   d. Set a date for one week from now to get together again and evaluate how successful your plan has been. If necessary, revise your plan at that time and repeat the process until you both feel that communication between you is improving.

FOOTNOTES

1. James G.T. Fairfield, **When You Don't Agree** (Scottdale, Pa.: Herald Press, 1977), p. 60.
2. Adapted from Sherod Miller, Elam W. Nunnally and Daniel B. Wackman, **Alive and Aware** (Minneapolis, Mn: Interpersonal Communication Programs, 1975), pp. 153-54.
3. Albert Metowbian, **Silent Messages** (Belmont, Calif.: Wadsworth Publishing Co., 1972) pp. 42-44.
4. H. Norman Wright, **Communication: Key to Your Marriage** (Glendale, Calif.: G/L Publications, Regal Books Div., 1974), pp. 58-60.

CHAPTER VIII

Put on Your Headphones

Jesus said, "He who has ears to hear, let him be listening, and consider and perceive and comprehend by hearing." Three times in the Gospel of Matthew Jesus made this statement (11:15; 13:9, 43, AMP). You and I are called upon to be listeners. There are hundreds of verses in the Scriptures that talk about hearing or being heard.

The Psalms reflect the listening and hearing qualities of God Himself. Psalm 34:15 and 17 says, "The eyes of the Lord are toward the righteous, and His ears are open to their cry . . . When the righteous cry for help, the Lord hears and delivers them out of all their distress and troubles" (AMP).

WHAT DO YOU THINK?

1. How would you define listening?

2. How would you describe your listening ability?

3. **How would your teenager describe your listening ability?**

Did you know that:

—One of the greatest complaints that adolescents mention is their parents do not listen to them?

—One of the major complaints made by parents about teenagers is the lack of listening and response they receive from them?

—Most people do not really know what is meant by listening nor have they received any training to become better listeners?

—The Scriptures command us to be ready listeners?

—If we are not totally open in our communication in our families we are not only limiting our relationships with one another but we will stifle our own Christian growth and our growth as members of the body of Christ?

TOTAL LISTENING

No one can accurately estimate the value of listening. As parents, one of the greatest gifts that we can give to our children is total listening. Paul Tournier put it this way: "How beautiful, how grand and liberating this experience is, when people learn to help each other. It is impossible to overemphasize the immense need humans have to be really listened to. Listen to all the conversation of our world, between nations as well as those between couples. They are, for the most part, dialogues of the deaf." [1]

Dr. S.I. Hayakawa said, "We can, if we are able to listen as well as to speak, become better informed and wiser as we grow older instead of being stuck like some people with the same little bundle of prejudices at 65 that we had at 25." [2]

"By consistently listening to a speaker, you are conveying the idea: 'I'm interested in you as a person, and I think that what you feel is important. I respect your thoughts, and even if I don't agree with them, I know that they are valid for you. I feel sure that you have a contribution to make. I'm not trying to change you or evaluate you. I just want to understand you. I think you're worth listening to, and I want you to know that I'm the kind of person that you can talk to.' " [3]

The Living Bible expresses these thoughts about listening: "What a shame—yes, how stupid!—to decide before knowing the facts" (Proverbs 18:13). "Any story sounds true until someone tells the other side and sets the record straight" (Proverbs 18:17). "The wise man learns by listening; the simpleton can learn only by seeing scorners punished" (Proverbs 21:11. "Let every man be quick to hear (a ready listener) . . ." (James 1:19, AMP).

What do we mean by listening? When we are listening to another person we are not thinking about what we are going to say when he stops talking. We are not busy formulating our response. We are concentrating on what is being said.

Do you ever listen with your answer running around inside, so that you are just bursting to let it fly? When your son or daughter is involved in sharing something with you, do you ever think that you know what is going to be said and complete the statement or question for the other person? To communicate, we don't have to answer for the other person. Nor do we have to formulate our own responses. All we have been asked to do is to patiently absorb and take in what is being shared. We may have a tendency to become angry or even threatened with what our teen is sharing, but we must hear him out.

Interrupting another person is another way of showing that we are not really listening. Interruptions can be verbal, but the nonverbal interruptions are even more annoying. The impatient look, the sigh, the wandering eyes, the crossing of the arms, the drumming fingers against the chair or table—all of these are basically saying, "Are you through? I'm not really listening and I want to talk."

This is one of the best opportunities that we will ever have to be welcomed into their world and experience it through their eyes! One of the ways in which we can show whether we are totally tuned in and giving full attention is how we listen with our bodies. Have you ever thought of how you listen with your hands? What do your hands say to your teen about your listening to them when they are sharing with you when you:

—Straighten up the room or rearrange the papers on the counter?
—Shuffle the pages of the paper or turn page after page of the magazine?
—Look around the room or shift your gaze from person to person or object to object?

When we use our hands or arms in listening we will find ourselves touching the other person or putting our arm around him. We can tell a person that we are ready and willing to be a listener (as it states in James 1:19) by stopping what we are doing and turning to him with our ears, our eyes, and the rest of our body. This is part of what we mean by total listening.

COMPLETE ACCEPTANCE

The second part of listening is this: Listening means we completely accept what is being shared without judging what is said or how it is stated. Often we fail to hear a message because we don't like the words that are used or the tone of voice.

If there is ever a time of life when a person may not speak properly or may overreact it is during the teen years. This is still a training period for them and if their speech is not as it should be, parents should not overreact or present a poor model for them to follow. It is possible to remain calm and in control and continue to listen. But you might be feeling, ''Well, I cannot accept what he is saying! I don't agree with him or I just don't like his tone of voice!''

What do we mean by acceptance? We do not mean that you have to agree with everything the other person is saying. We mean that you understand that what is being shared is what the other person believes or feels. Your listening is sharing part of his life at that point. It does not mean that you feel or believe that way nor do you have to agree!

Acceptance does not mean approval. There is a difference that is important. Approval might be, ''Don't pay any attention to what they say. They don't know you that well. I think you did what was right. Why feel bad about it?'' Acceptance is, ''I'm not sure I can agree with all you have said but I am glad you felt free enough to share that with me. I care about you as a person and I hope I can convey that to you even when we don't see eye to eye.''

Also involved in this part of the definition of listening is that it is more important for us as parents to understand than to analyze! Analysis is: ''I know what's bothering you. I know what the trouble is. Now sit down and listen to me. Here's the trouble . . .'' Understanding on the other hand involves this: ''You know, I think I'm starting to see what you're going through. I guess you might be feeling left out, is that it? I'm starting to imagine what that is like.''

As parents it is so easy to want to jump in and offer suggestions or correction as we are afraid that our teen is going to make a mistake, get into difficulty or exercise some wrong judgment. But if we hear him out we may find that he has resources we haven't given him credit for. Can you wait until your teen asks you for your analysis or opinion?

But what about the times you feel it is vital to express an opinion? Opinions are important and so are judgments. So it is important to make a distinction between a judgment and disapproval. This is a very fine distinction to make, however. Disapproval might be like, ''I don't like what you are doing and you had better stop. It isn't right and it's going to have an effect upon our relationship.'' Judgment might be like, ''You know, I believe in you as a person but I also feel that what you are doing is wrong. I could be mistaken but that is how I feel and this is why.''

Judgment comes after the process of listening, however. We weigh the information and **then** make the judgment. This is not unusual for God does this.

God **listens** to us and hears us; then He responds in love and makes a judgment.

FULL UNDERSTANDING

There is yet a third part of the process of total listening. If we have truly listened then we should be able to repeat what the other person has said with full understanding. We should be able to explain what we think he was feeling when he expressed it. This means that we have to move into the other person's world and sense what he is saying from his perspective.

Hearing is not enough! You can hear without really listening. As one husband expressed it to his wife, "Of course I hear you. I don't have to listen to you to hear you!"

DERAILING THE LISTENING PROCESS

There are several major distractors to the process of listening.

One distractor is that sometimes we do not care enough to want to know what is going on in our teenager's life. Listening is a form of loving and really caring. This is one of the ways God expresses His caring for us—through listening.

Another reason why we do not listen as we should is that our teenager may be expressing things that we do not want to hear. So we tune him out and put our mind on automatic pilot. Perhaps someone has reacted to you in this way. You shared with him previously about a subject, then when you bring it up again he says, "You never said that. You're wrong. You never once talked about that. I remember." Well, you did talk about it but he had his filter system on and just tuned you out. If this ever happens to you repeat what you said and ask if he understands. If sometimes you do this, ask the other person to repeat what he said.

One of the main reasons that we have difficulty listening is that physiologically we can listen five times as fast as we can speak. If you can listen at 400 words a minute and your teen is speaking at 120 words a minute, this extra capacity is distracted from the speaker and you may become bored or prepare your rebuttal.

The message system of communication may be a distractor to total listening. Specialists say that when you talk with another person there are actually six messages that can come through:

1. What you mean to say.
2. What you actually say.
3. What your teenager hears.
4. What the teenager thinks he hears.
5. What the teenager says about what you said.
6. What you think the teenager said about what you said.

INCREASING YOUR LISTENING ABILITY

Any one of these listening distractors may be the reason why we have listening problems! What can you do now? How can you increase your listening ability? You can listen with your ears, eyes, and your total body. Observe your teenager when he is talking. Look at him. Listen to his tone of voice and his feelings as he shares with you.

Don't interrupt. Concentrate on what your teenager is saying at this point in time and don't recall other conversations which might affect how you listen. Don't hurry him. You might be one who speaks at 200 words a minute and he speaks at 80, but let him proceed at his own pace.

Create an atmosphere for listening. What do you do when your teenager arrives home from school or from an outing? Do you constantly give the message that you are not available for talking? Do you ever come into his room and, sprawl on the bed and listen to his new record (even though it sends you up the wall!)?

If you ask him, "What's wrong," and he says "nothing," or, "it doesn't matter," do you let him know that you're interested if he would like to talk? Do you ever shut off the TV or the radio so you can really listen to him without any distractions? As a former youth pastor I discovered that one of the best times to listen to the kids and learn what was going on in their lives was when I drove a car full of them somewhere. I didn't say much but just listened to their conversations.

PREPARE YOURSELF FOR LISTENING

When your teenager does want to talk with you be sure that you give him your full attention. Turn off any distracting elements such as the blender, vacuum cleaner, power saw, TV, etc. Set aside what you are doing or holding in your hand as this says, "I'm ready to listen to you."

It helps to pick some appropriate times when you want to talk with him. If you are really too busy, let him know that you will set aside time at 7:00 to listen to him and you won't let any one else interrupt you at this point. Above all, be willing to hear his hurts and upsets.

WHAT'S YOUR PLAN?

1. List three specific behaviors you will either change or begin during this next week in order to improve your listening ability.

   1. _____

   2. _____

   3. _____

2. How do you expect your teenager to respond if you are consistent in doing this?
3. What will a pattern of better listening do for you as a person?
4. Describe an experience in which you felt God really listened to you.
5. Memorize Proverb 18:13 and James 1:19.

FOOTNOTES

1. Paul Tournier, **To Understand Each Other** (Richmond, Va.: John Knox Press, 1967), p. 29
2. S.I. Hayakawa—original source unknown.
3. George E. and Nikki Koehler, **My Family: How Shall I Live With It** (Chicago: Rand McNally & Co., 1968), p. 57.

CHAPTER IX

Guidelines for Communication

GUIDELINE ONE

One of the healthiest models of clear communication was presented in the Minnesota Couples Communication Program. This model, called "Skill for Expressing Self-Awareness," is presented here and adapted to the parent-teen relationship. The four skills include:

1. Speaking for self rather than for others
2. Documenting with descriptive behavioral data
3. Making feeling statements (speaking about oneself)
4. Making intention statements (speaking about oneself)

Speaking for Self

Father: "I'd like to go to the ball game tonight."
Teenager: "Hey, that's a great idea. I'd like to go too. I'd like to sit in the bleachers too. What about you?"
Father: "I think that's a good idea."

In this example both father and teenager are sharing what they think and feel.

Some underresponsible people don't like to let

others know what they think or feel. They speak indirectly, often making sweeping generalizations about what "everyone" thinks or feels:

Parent: "Some parents would really be angry if their teenager came in at 2 a.m."

Teenager: "Are you mad or something?"

Parent: "No. I'm not, but some parents would be!"

This type of person is trying to avoid being open about his own thoughts, feelings, or intentions. Often he denies his anger, thoughts, concern, or intentions.

The overresponsible parent also leaves out the "I." This person tries to speak for others. He tells them what they think or feel or intend by sending "you messages."

"You don't like that kind of TV program. Let's turn it to something else."

"You're not feeling well, are you?"

"You probably want to go out with your friends again tonight."

A close variation of speaking for yourself is called the "I message." This type of message identifies what the parent feels and thinks. The parent may want to modify the behavior of the teenager, to change a situation, or simply to identify what he believes or feels. An "I message" is distinguished from a "you message" in that the speaker claims the problem as his own. A true "I message" has three parts: the feeling, the situation, and how it effects the person speaking. It is a statement of fact rather than an evaluation of the other person's thoughts or feelings. This type of communication models honesty and openness.

Documenting with Descriptive Behavioral Data

Document what you say with descriptive behavioral information. This means give a description: "John, I think you're happy today. You're tripping around here whistling and you've got a smile on your face. What's going on with you right now?"

Documenting is important because it increases your own understanding of yourself. It gives you a better idea of how you arrived at your own thoughts and feelings, and it gives the other person a much clearer idea of what your are responding to in his life.

Making Feeling Statements

Make feeling statements. When you make a feeling statement you don't know how the other person will respnd, so in a sense these statements are risky.

Mother: "I feel upset when I see you lying around the house doing nothing."

Father: "I feel angry when it appears that I'm not being listened to."

Making Intention Statements

Making intention statements is a way of expressing your immediate goals or desires in a situation. These statements provide a different kind of self-information to the other person—an overview of what you are willing to do.

Father: "I sure would like to end this arguement."

Teenager: "I didn't know that. I thought you were going to go on and on and were too mad to stop."

Mother: "I would like for us to take some time

	and sit down and share where all of us would like to go on vacation this year.''
Teenager:	''I'd like that. Usually I don't have any voice in that and I would really like to share some ideas too.''

Intention statements are usually surprising because so often people think they know what the other's intentions are. But do we?

WHAT DO YOU THINK?

Earlier we talked about ''I messages.'' It is important to practice these and other communication skills to make them a part of our life. Take time now to complete this exercise. Change the ''You messages'' into ''I messages.''

Situation	You message	I message
Mother picks up empty glasses from the rug in the family room for the fourth morning in a row.	''You left your glass in the family room again for the fourth time. You are certainly forgetful and messy.''	
The teenager comes home with two new records. He and his parents had decided that this month he would not spend any extra money.	''You have no concept of how to handle money. You just throw it away and never save a dime. What had we decided?''	
The teenager has been picking on		

his younger brothers and has been teasing them for an hour.	"You are being cruel to them. What's the matter with you?"
Mother discovers some strange look- ing cigarettes in her son's room.	"You've been smok- ing grass! How could you do this to yourself and us? You're going to turn into a dope fiend."

GUIDELINE TWO

Show trust in the comments or statements of your teenagers. Too many teenagers have said that living in their home is like serving a jail sentence or being continually on trial. They feel like they are contin- ually looked upon as guilty and have to prove their innocence. Many parents do look upon their teen- agers as guilty until proven innocent instead of inno- cent until proven guilty. Again, we must be willing to trust even when our trust is violated at times. James Fairfield said this about trust in the parent-teen relationship:

"But what if a son—or daughter—doesn't earn your trust? What if your trust is betrayed? David Augsburger explores this in his book, **The Love Fight.** 'I can't trust you anymore,' parents often say. That's not true. The word 'can't' is false. 'I won't trust you anymore' would be a more honest state- ment.

" 'Can't' is an irresponsible word. It says, 'Your actions make it impossible for me and I can do nothing—I am not responsible.' When you change the words 'I can't' to 'I won't' the truth begins to surface bringing responsibility with it.

"You might try something like this: 'Yes, I trust you to use your best judgment. But I know from my own experience that one person's best judgment may not include quite enough important facts of knowledge to be completely dependable. And sometimes it may need buttressing with some help from others— even parents. If it's important to you that we trust you to use your best judgment, will you trust us to use our best judgment in the questions we raise and the suggestions we make?' " [1]

WHAT DO YOU THINK?

1. **Write three examples of comments that you could make to convey trust to your teenager.**

2. **What does your teenager say or do to show he trusts you?**

GUIDELINE THREE

Be an encourager, not a criticizer. Accusations lead us to the area of criticism. Criticism does not build others up; it tears them down. Often criticism is a response from us because we are hurt or frustrated.

The Word of God has an answer for this: "Stop being so critical of one another. If you must be critical, be critical of yourself and see that you do not cause your brother to stumble" (Romans 14:13, PHIL). The Scripture also tells us to "encourage one another" (1 Thessalonians 5:14).

Dr. Sven Wahlroos has suggested, " . . . criticism must be discriminate and take into account the fact that no human being is perfect and that there are many matters which are so unimportant that they should be ignored . . . When criticism becomes indiscriminate it is called faultfinding and it leads to most destructive consequences . . .

"(These) are the factors which make faultfinding so destructive . . .

"1. Faultfinding is destructive because of its very definition . . . Faultfinding expresses a lack of acceptance of people and a distorted view of reality.

"2. Because of the basic lack of acceptance involved, faultfinding ruins human relationships, makes people feel hostile toward each other, sours the daily atmosphere of the home and makes it a place of misery rather than of happiness and satisfaction.

"3. Faultfinding is destructive not only to the 'victims' (many of whom are not as innocent as it may appear), but to the faultfinder himself or herself, as well. That is because faultfinding makes the other person either turn you off completely, counterattack or store up resentment against you . . .

"4. It follows that faultfinding is an ineffective method for changing the behavior of others. It may produce initial results, but if it is kept up it will lead to the other person not really hearing what you are saying; he may hear it in a mechanical sense but it will soon 'go out through the other ear.' Rest assured, however, that the lack of acceptance involved is received and understood.

"5. Thus, faultfinding can be dangerous because when the time comes that you have a truly necessary and important criticism to make, you are powerless then, having diluted the effectiveness of your arguments in advance so that they no longer mean anything to the person being criticized. The danger is especially apparent in the case of children who—through faultfinding—have been taught to think: 'Never mind, it's just that cranky old parent-faultfinder putting on his broken record again.'

"6. Faultfinding teaches unreasonableness and intolerance. Since it induces distaste, it may lead the other party (spouse, child, employee, etc.) to become unreasonable in the other extreme by becoming especially careless and making an excessive number of mistakes, thus setting up a neurotic interaction . . .

"7. Faultfinding is a consequence of reliance on certain destructive defense mechanisms. The typical faultfinder either projects his own shortcomings onto another person or displaces his anger toward one person (e.g., boss) onto another (e.g., wife). Most often, faultfinding is an unconscious way of trying to hide one's own weaknesses by projecting them onto someone else . . ." [2]

WHAT DO YOU THINK?

1. **How could you share a complaint with your teen- ager so that it isn't a criticism or faultfinding?**

GUIDELINE FOUR

Be truthful with your questions. Avoid questions that are not really questions. Have you ever been asked a question like "When are you going to start listening to me?" or "When are you ever going to do what I ask you to do?" or "When are you going to stop running around with these idiots?" What are these so-called "questions" really saying? They sound more like traps, demands to change, put-downs. Is the questioner really asking a question and looking for an answer?

WHAT DO YOU THINK?

Look at the question "When are you ever going to do what I ask you to do?" What is this really saying? Take a moment and write down what this implies.

This statement could be saying, "You don't do anything right. You had better change."

A real question is one that probes for facts or feelings, looks for information, or asks for observations of feelings and values. An unreal question is one that limits information, makes demands, tries to control, and doesn't really exhibit trust of the other person.

The **leading** question attempts to contain or limit the responses of the other person. It also attempts to guide or lead him or manipulate the direction he takes. "Don't you think that . . .?" "Isn't it true that . . .?" "Wouldn't you prefer . . .?"

The **punishing** question challenges the other's opinions, rights, and intelligence. "Why did you do . . .?" "Why did you say . . .?" "Why didn't you try . . .?"

The **hypothetical** question is an interesting one. It is sometimes used to criticize another person's behavior or ideas by suggesting your own, and of course yours is better. "Wouldn't you rather do it this way if you were in charge?" "If you were going out with her wouldn't you think this would be best . . .?"

The **command** question is no question at all but a dictation in disguise. "Why don't you see if . . ." "When are you going to . . ."

The **trap** question is sometimes called "the set-up." It is phrased in such a way that the one answering seems to convict himself with his own words. "Is it true that you . . .?"

Why do we ask questions? What is our purpose? Is it for the other person to have an opportunity to openly respond with his feelings and thoughts? When we ask a question we need to be willing to hear the response, even a response that goes against what we really wanted to hear. Sometimes parents ask their teenagers, "Wouldn't you like to go along and visit so and so with us?" When they respond, "No," we become angry. Why should we become angry if we are truly asking if they **want** to go? Do they have the right to say "Yes" or "No," or do we want to program them so they respond only according to our wishes? Speaking the truth in love and not lying to one another as the scripture says involves our questions as well.

SILENT SAM

Is your teenager a silent Sam? Does he pull the silent treatment or is he usually in a noncommunicative mood? This is a frequent gripe and concern of many parents. Many have said, "I would love to communicate but how can you with a brick wall!" If your teenager fits this description, ask yourself the question, what is his silence saying? What is the message behind the silence? It could communicate love, satisfaction, well-being, pouting, sulking, indifference, hostility, bitterness, or fear.

WHAT DO YOU THINK?

What does your silence mean to you and to others? What does your teenager's silence mean to him and what does it mean to you?

What can you do to help the silent member open up? Saying "talk to me" usually doesn't help. Ask for opinions and avoid questions that can be responded with a "yep" or "nope." Ask "What do you think about . . .?'' or ''What would you suggest . . .?'' If he says, ''I don't know,'' you could offer three or four suggestions.

Some parents have used other statements such as ''I wonder what you are trying to say to me by being silent'' or ''I wonder if there is something that I am doing that makes it hard for you to talk with me.'' Be willing to listen if he responds with ''Well, now that you've asked, there is something.'' Don't put pressure on your teenager. You might say, ''I am willing to talk with you so when you feel that you would like to talk, let me know.'' Then back off, pray for an abundance of patience, and wait.

HOW'S YOUR HUMOR QUOTIENT?

Humor can clear the air and bring relief from tension and anxiety or it can create hostile reactions in your teenager. The phrase ''I was just kidding, can't you take a joke?'' can be a sore spot if a teenager hears it too often from his parents. Proverbs warns, ''As a madman who casts firebrands, arrows and death, so is the man who deceives his neighbor and then says, 'Was I not joking?' '' (Proverbs 26:18-19, AMP).

Using humor flippantly when your teenager is depressed or discouraged will deepen the discouragement. He may believe that you don't care and that you can't see the problem from his perspective. Humor and joking have their place, but timing is very important. Proverbs 15:23 states, ''A man has joy in making an apt answer, and a word spoken at the right moment, how good it is!'' (AMP).

Humor can be used as a weapon if we constantly make the other person the goal of the jokes or if we use joking to make ourselves look good or appear superior. Sarcasm, ridicule, and flippancy are destructive under most circumstances.

Some teenagers have complained that their parents are never serious enough to have a discussion. They especially don't want a comedian around to cheer them up after a breakup with a girl or boy friend or after a setback in school. But neither do they appreciate the "great stoneface" who never cracks a smile.

Parents can put a damper on an atomosphere by being overly serious and concerned. A balance must be maintained.

There are many bright spots in life, and perhaps our teenager can help us see them if we view life through his eyes with him.

WHAT IS YOUR PLAN?

1. **Read back over the specific Communication Guidelines in this chapter. Number them in order of which ones need to be improved most in your own communication pattern.**

   ___ 1. **Speaking for yourself.**
   ___ 2. **Document with descriptive behavioral data**
   ___ 3. **Make feeling statements**
   ___ 4. **Make intention statements**
   ___ 5. **Using "I" messages**
   ___ 6. **Showing trust in statements**
   ___ 7. **Be an encourager**
   ___ 8. **Be truthful with your questions**
   ___ 9. **Pressuring when your teenager is silent**
   ___10. **Using humor constructively**

2. Which three of the above would your teenager suggest that you improve?

3. Describe what you will do for the next week to bring about positive changes.

FOOTNOTES

1. James Fairfield, **When You Don't Agree** (Scottdale, Pa.: Herald Press, 1977), pp. 116-117.
2. Sven Wahlroos, **Family Communication** (New York: Macmillan, 1974), pp. 20-21.

CHAPTER X

Constructive Creative Conflict

"You've got to be kidding! Conflict can be creative and constructive? Not around our place! It sounds like we're doing a tune-up for World War III!"

Does that sound like your family life? Does the idea of conflict being creative sound incredible to you? Incredible or not, it is true. Instead of being a shattering disaster, conflict can be a positive growing experience.

One dictionary definition of conflict is "1) to strike together; 2) a fight, clash or contention; 3) sharp disagreement such as interests, ideas, etc."

Thomas Gordon, who developed Parent Effectiveness Training, described conflict as the "moment of truth in a relationship—a test of its health which can either weaken or strengthen it. Conflicts can push people away from each other or pull them closer together."

Why does conflict occur? The answer is simply that we are human beings and therefore imperfect people. Each of us has our own desires, wants, needs, and goals. Whenever any of these stand up against those of another person, conflict occurs.

Our differences in beliefs, ideas, attitudes, feelings, and behavior are natural, and so are the conflicts that result from these differences. We often look at other family members and say, "You do everything differently. You think differently, act differently, and approach things differently. What is wrong with you?" Why do we believe that differences are necessarily wrong?

Paul Fairfield said, "We were created as irreplaceable individuals, different from all who have gone before or who will appear again. This is a frightening thought to insecure people who have not realized that God considers each person to be a talented individual of unique worth." [1]

Another cause of conflict is a struggle for independence. The Revolutionary War, fought many years ago over individuals' needs and desires for independence, is refought many times each day between parents and teenagers. We as parents often have a difficult time letting go. Just as newborn infants automatically know how to grasp but must learn how to let go, so parents must learn how to let go and allow their teenagers to be independent.

Not getting our own way also leads to conflict. "What causes conflicts and quarrels among you? Do they not spring from the aggressiveness of your bodily desires? You want something which you cannot have, and so you are bent on murder; you are envious, and cannot attain your ambition, and so you quarrel and fight. You do not get what you want, because you do not pray for it. Or, if you do, your requests are not granted because you pray from wrong motives" (James 4:1-3, NEB).

We can minimize conflict by learning to apply Ephesians 4:2 to our lives, especially the latter portion. "Living as becomes you—with complete lowliness of mind (humility) and meekness (unselfishness, gentleness, mildness), with patience, bearing with one another and making allowances because you love one another" (AMP).

WHAT DO YOU THINK?

1. Describe some recent or current conflicts between you and your teen.

2. Who do you believe caused the conflict? What was the outcome? What did it accomplish, good or bad?

3. How did you create or contribute to the conflict?

4. Imagine that you are seeing the conflict from the other person's perspective. How would he describe it? Who was responsible and what was accomplished?

5. **If you could go through the same conflict again, how would you handle it this time?**

Here are some basic points to remember about conflicts.

Conflict is a natural part of growth and family living; it is inevitable. Our perceptions allow for different opinions and choices. People grow, change, and develop.

Have you ever thought that many conflicts are simply symptoms of something else? We often see a conflict as "the" problem, but in reality it is not. Solving the "conflict" does not solve the problem. Look below the symptom to see what it represents. A teenager asking for permission to stay out later at night or to use the car more may reflect his need for more freedom and independence rather than an actual desire for driving or staying out.

Another true but sad fact is that most individuals do not deal openly with conflict because no one has ever taught them effective ways of dealing with it. Too many families ignore minor conflicts to keep from rocking the boat. We avoid other conflicts because of the lack of necessary and basic skills.

On the positive side, conflict provides opportunity for growth in a relationship. Conflict is like dynamite. It can be helpful if used in the right way but can also be destructive if used at the wrong time and in the wrong manner.

Unresolved and buried conflicts arise from their coffin and interfere with growth and satisfying relationships. Barriers are erected and are reinforced with an increasing dependence upon defensiveness.

What choices do we have in dealing with conflicts? James Fairfield has suggested five styles of dealing with conflict. [2] The first is to **withdraw**. If you have a tendency to view conflict as a hopeless inevitability which you can do little to control, you may not even try. You may withdraw physically by leaving the scene or you may leave psychologically.

If you feel that you must always look after your own interests, or if your self-concept is threatened in a conflict, you may choose the second style, which is to **win**. No matter what the cost, you must win! Domination is usually reflected in this style; personal relationships take second place.

While driving along the highway or approaching an intersection you have probably noticed a **yield** sign. "Giving in to get along" is the third style. You don't like it, but rather than risk a continuing confrontation you eventually choose this path.

"Give a little to get a little" is called **compromise**, the fourth style. You may find that it is important to let up on some of your demands or ideas in order to help the other person give a little. You don't want to win all the time nor do you want the other person to win all the time.

Fifth, a person may choose to **resolve** conflicts. In this style of dealing with conflicts a situation, attitude, or behavior is changed by open and direct communication.

WHAT DO YOU THINK?

1. **Which style is your basic approach to conflict?**

2. **How does your style affect the feeling of others toward you?**

3. **How does it affect your feelings about yourself?**

What style did Jesus use? What styles of handling conflict do we find in the Scriptures? Take a few minutes and read the following accounts of conflict. Try to determine the methods used at that time. John 8:1-11; Genesis 4 (Cain and Abel); I Samuel 20:30-34; Matthew 15:10-20; John 11:11-19. Write down the various styles you observed.

Which style is best for your family life?

High concern for relationship

Yield	Resolve
Low in achieved needs	Compromise	High in achieved needs
Withdraw	Win

Low concern for relationship

As you can see from the diagram[3] above, **withdraw** has the lowest value because the person gives up on meeting the goals and on developing the relationship. If this style is used temporarily as a cooling off step toward **resolve**, it is beneficial. There may be times when the discussion is so heated and out of control that withdrawing is best. But it is important to make a definite and specific commitment to discuss and resolve the conflict.

The **win** method achieves the goal but can sacrifice the relationship. In a family, personal relationships are just as important or even more important than the goal.

Yielding works just the other way in that the relationship is maintained but the goals are sacrificed.

Compromise attempts to work out some needs but the bargaining involved may mean that you compromise some of your own values.

Naturally the highest value or style is **resolve** because in the final analysis relationships are strengthened as you seek to meet personal needs.

How then can we proceed to the resolving of conflict? Consider trying (again and again) and applying these principles.

1. When a conflict arises, instead of demanding that you be heard, listen carefully to the other person (see Proverbs 18:13 and James 1:19). Any changes that another person wants to see in another must be heard and understood. If you as a parent are a true listener, your teenager will be more prone to listen to you.

2. Select an appropriate time. "A man has joy in making an apt answer, and a word spoken at the right moment, how good it is" (Proverbs 15:23, AMP). Trying to solve conflicts on the run, while doing dishes, walking out to the car, or when you are hungry or physically exhausted, is courting disaster. Of course some conflicts must he handled on the spot, but not all of them. Select a time when those involved have time and interruptions can be eliminated.

3. Define the problem. How do you define the problem and how does the other person? What behaviors had led to or contributed to this problem? What behaviors does your teen feel have contributed to the difficulty?

4. Define the areas of agreement and disagreement in the conflict. Don't generalize and say that there are no areas of agreement. Most of the time there are, but we overlook them and make the problem loom larger than it is!

5. Here comes the difficult part. A few conflicts **may** be just one sided, but most involve contributions from both sides. Identify your own contribution to the problem. When you accept some responsibility for a problem, the other person sees a willingness to cooperate and will probably be much more open to the discussion.

Don't blame, attack, or ridicule the other person. This doesn't mean that you don't talk about his behavior. You do, but not in an attacking manner. Share something like ''John, I feel that I haven't always understood what you want and haven't always listened as closely as I should have'' or ''John, I feel that I have been asking you to do too much'' or ''I feel that I have been nagging you about this.''

In stating what you feel about his behavior, be precise and specific and share what it is about his behavior or attitude that you find acceptable. Be sure that you share what behaviors the other person feels are probably unacceptable on your part too.

6. The next step is to state positively what behaviors on your part would probably help and to be willing to ask for his opinion. As he shares with you, be open to his feelings, observations, and suggestions. Watch out for defensiveness! It would be well to memorize the following to help lower the edge of defensiveness.

''If you refuse criticism you will end in poverty and disgrace; if you accept criticism you are on the road to fame'' (Proverbs 13:18, TLB).

''Don't refuse to accept criticism; get all the help you can'' (Proverbs 23:12, TLB).

It is a badge of honor to accept valid criticism'' (Proverbs 25:12, TLB).

"A man who refuses to admit his mistakes can never be successful. But if he confesses and forsakes them, he gets another chance'' (Proverbs 28:13, TLB).

Offer him a positive suggestion that you would appreciate seeing in his life as a means of resolving the conflict. But offer suggestions with a nonthreatening tone in your voice. As you talk together perhaps both of you can suggest some alternatives. This is the time for individual and joint brainstorming. Each person should think of as many solutions to the problem as possible. The posing of several solutions is very important as the greater the number, the more likely you will find one that both of you will respond to and accept.

7. Make a commitment to follow these new solutions. Your commitment is not based, however, on what your teenager decides to do. He may decide not to change or change in a way that you don't expect or like. But that shouldn't stop you from developing a new healthy style of your own for resolving conflict. One of the questions to continually ask yourself is this: Is what I am doing now getting what I want? If not, why keep doing it? There must be a better way.

WHAT'S YOUR PLAN?

1. This week if a conflict arises in our family I will___

---

2. A conflict other family members would like my help in resolving is _____
_____

3. Three possible alternatives to this conflict are:

   1. _____

   2. _____

   3. _____

4. If I were to choose:

   1. _____

   2. _____

   3. _____

   My family members would _____
   _____

5. In order for our family to sit down and pray together about our conflicts I would have to _____
_____
_____

FOOTNOTES

1. James G.T. Fairfield, **When You Don't Agree: A Guide to Resolving Marriage and Family Conflict** (Scottdale, Pa.: Herald Press, 1977), p. 19.
2. Ibid, p. 149.
3. Ibid, p. 231.

CHAPTER XI

Dressing, Driving, Dialing, Dating

Let's look now at four issues around which many parent-teen problems revolve. Rarely are they a problem in and of themselves. More often, conflicts in these areas indicate other more important problems such as trust, the growth of responsibility and the development and maintenance of communication. But each of these issues need to be considered because they represent problem areas for many families.

CONFRONTING THE ISSUES

There are two traps to avoid when confronting issues such as dressing, dialing, driving and dating. One is that of oversimplifying; and the other is that of complicating the issue. Parents can complicate the situation by seeing each issue as a major disturbance.

Oversimplifying the issues is more of a trap that writers and preachers get into. Pigeonholing behaviors and delivering pat answers make for neat outlines but are rarely helpful in finding long range solutions. The parent-trap in this case is applying "easy" solutions to your own family without careful consideration of each teenager's differences and needs.

In confronting the issues in this chapter as well as other issues, there are two basic principles that are helpful.

First, act instead of reacting. It is natural for all people—parents and teenagers included, to notice change and overlook the familiar. You get a new suit or tie, and get several comments on how good you look. Of course if you do this regularly, people get used to seeing you in new clothes so you're not noticed as much.

One of the most important tasks of adolescence is finding an identity. Part of the process of finding an identity is trying on different identities to see how they fit. It is almost like trying on different kinds of clothes. it is a trial-and-error process that focuses on alternatives. A lot of experimentation is going to go on.

As our teenagers work at finding their own identities by experimenting with new looks, sounds, ideas, friends, experiences, beliefs and values, the first thing parents notice is all the change. Now we have to deal with the urge to protect our teenagers because we love them. We know what has worked for us. We know some of the pitfalls, the traps, and the costs of falling into them. So naturally, we get uptight when we see our son or daughter approaching one. We react, sometimes vehemently, and rather than rewarding our love and concern, our teenagers accuse us of selfishness and indifference.

If we can act, instead of reacting to change when we notice it, we can give ourselves time to consider the alternatives. This means stifling the urge to comment on our daughter's new see-through blouse, the acid rock record, the dent in the front fender or the boy with the long hair. Acting means we take time to think, to talk it over as parents, to ask questions, and most importantly, to reflect on alternative responses to the situation. Then when we do respond to our teenager's new behavior we do so on our own initiative, after having considered our own feelings.

This is sometimes hard to do because teenagers often try a new idea, apparel, experience or belief just to see how their parents will react. This is evidence of concern for their relationship with their parents. So a carefully considered response demonstrates your concern for your relationship too.

Second, watch for patterns. Do you react to every change or every request with an automatic "no"? Is your pattern of response predictable? Maybe your response is one of resignation—you can't control the inevitable. Maybe your response is always positive—and you sometimes wonder if you're too permissive. Maybe your response is usually a "maybe." Is there a pattern? It could be a vacillating pattern or a pendular one—you come down hard on your teenager for something you consider outrageous and then you feel guilty, so you avoid saying "no" to anything he does for a while.

DRESSING

The clothes your teenager picks and the way your teenager styles and manages his or her hair are important indicators of self-image. And dress tends to be one of the first issues that arise in families. A fifth or sixth grader who has gone along with his parents' choice of clothes turns into a junior high freak on one trip to the shopping mall. What's happening? Your growing adolescent is finding ways to express his changing self.

How do you respond to outlandish costumes? Some parents see young people wearing clothes they hope their kids won't ever wear, and fearing they might be attracted to these costumes, they make very negative comments about them. Other parents react violently when their own teenagers show up in one of these costumes. If you avoid patterns and reacting, you're gong to find some alternate ways of responding.

One of these alternatives is based on the truth that we all choose our clothes and appearance to express or advertise ourselves. Some men advertise themselves as businessmen by the suit and tie they choose. Women's apparel and makeup are deliberately designed to "accent" or "hide," to "round and shape," to "lift and separate" to advertise certain features a woman considers important.

Teenagers' clothes are made and chosen to advertise too. T-shirts and sweatshirts even use pictures and words to advertise the ideas, philosophy or wants of their wearers. One way, then, to respond to the new clothes your son or daughter brings home is to ask, "What are you trying to advertise about yourself?" "Is that what you want to advertise?" Whatever your teenagers' answers are, be ready to accept what they say about themselves.

WHAT DO YOU THINK?

1. **What are you advertising by the clothes and appearance you choose?**

2. What other aspects of your personality could be accented by a change in a style of dress or appearance?

3. What message are you receiving from your teenagers about themselves by the clothes and appearance they choose?

4. If you were to choose and buy your teenager an outfit, what would your purchase tell you about your wishes for them?

_____

DIALING

Do you associate the word "dialing" with your telephone, your television, your radio or your stereo? Most families have to deal with the issue of dialing with at least one of these instruments as the focus. Maybe your dialing conflict is over the telephone. Your adolescent seems to feel that the phone is God's answer to their energy crisis, and any limitation on telephone time is a form of cruel and unusual punishment.

Maybe it's the radio or stereo that are issues in your home. If the unbearably loud music (noise?) doesn't get to you, the constant sight of headphones sprouting like growths on the sides of your teenagers head does. You're not sure whether it's music or some electrical paralysis sedating his mind. The effect is that he slowly becomes a zombie, reluctant to do anything but listen to his records or radio. Or maybe your teenager is a TV addict. Some teenagers spend over thirty hours per week staring at the tube.

Is this another sign of identity formation? It could be, but not neccessarily. If a teenager has a low level of self-esteem, he or she may be spending lots of time on the telephone getting reassurance from friends that he is a valued person. On the other hand, an inordinate numbers of hours in front of the television or listening to albums may also be a symptom of ''identity diffusion.''

Identity diffusion is the inability to put together an acceptable identity. One writer on adolescence describes it as ''an inability to define himself, to relate sexually with others, to decide on an occupation, to engage in competition with his peers or with adults—any one or a combination of these . . .''[1] The decisions an adolescent faces are important to him, yet he is afraid to make them. The result is that he experiences feelings of alienation and shame. So he loses those feelings in the mind-numbing comfort of TV and records.

A second possible reason for overuse of the phone, TV, stereo or radio may simply be that it is a selfish habit. A teenager may be so involved in his own friendships and interests that there is a failure to consider the needs of others in the family.

Some families resolve the "dialing issue," by providing their teenager with their own phone, stereo and T.V. These are not only expensive, they usually have the effect of banishing the teenager from his family, to his room. This strategy can actually build alienation. Buying a teenager his own dialing instruments may be a quick and convenient way of solving immediate issues, but opportunities for growth may also be lost. It is in the resolution of conflicts that people grow, not in avoidance.

Some families resolve the issues by appeal to the family's line of authority. Sociologists call this line a "pecking order," and it is often well illustrated by conflict over the use of the phone, the TV or the stereo. In this system the father (head of the home) has the most rights to the family's resources as well as the "last word." So if anyone else is watching TV and he wants to watch it, he just turns the dial to his program (football) and the rest of the family can either watch it with him or go do something else. The mother in this system is second in command and then the children in order of descending age. The "line of authority" may work for some families, but it turns out to be a poor way of teaching children and adolescents to prefer one another in honor. It is a better way to teach social role expectations than love and esteem.

If dialing is an issue in your family, let's suggest another way of dealing with the issues—a way that hopefully will help you communicate and respond more easily with each other. This idea, which a lot of families use, is to build a "dialing covenant." A dialing covenant is a promise worked out by the whole family, written down and signed by the whole family. It is different from most "family rules" in that the whole family negotiates the covenant rather than being solely decreed by the parents. Also it is written down and signed to avoid misunderstanding. Third, everyone's accountability is to the whole family, not just to parents, and parents are expected to live up to their covenant as much as are teenagers.

To set up a dialing contract, dad needs to take the initiative and call a family council when there is plenty of time to talk. He might then suggest that to resolve conflict over the use of the phone, the TV and/or the stereo that the family work on a covenant. He can then describe what a covenant is, using the description in this chapter if needed, and then accept suggestions. It is important that everyone concerned be involved.

The following "What do you think?" questions should help you put together a dialing covenant.

WHAT DO YOU THINK?

1. **Do you need a statement of purpose to begin your dialing covenant? You might start with "It is our purpose as a family to** _____

   _____

   _____

2. Would a weekly planning meeting to schedule dialing time fit your family style? Some families make weekly planning (including scanning their TV Guide) a regular part of their family night home.

3. Would a sign-up sheet be a helpful tool?

4. Would a telephone log be a helpful tool?

5. Are there certain chores or homework that must be done before the stereo or TV may be turned on or the phone used?

6. What about watching TV or listening to albums with friends? Does their presence change the schedule?

7. Do you want to make a limit on total TV, stereo or phone time?

DRIVING

Driving becomes an issue for almost every family some time prior to the age each state sets for minimum eligibility. The ability to drive is a major milestone, in our society, on the road to personal independence. Psychologically, it is the equivalent of puberty rites in other societies. The driver's license distinguishes the ''high school adults'' from the ''junior high kids.''

Acquisition of a driver's license can be a time of growth, especially in responsibility, or it can be a time of regression to playing with new toys; only the toys can now kill. So planning for driving is an area that both parents and teenagers can and should invest in early—at least six months before eligibility to drive. If you start developing a driving contract with your teenager's suggestions, you're less likely to incur the feeling that you're imposing a set of restrictions.

What if your teenagers are already driving, and the way they drive, the places they drive too, or their lack of returning home before agreed deadlines are issues? If these behaviors are occurring regularly your teenagers are misplacing your trust and demonstrating their lack of readiness for the responsibility of driving.

WHAT DO YOU THINK?

1. **Is your teenager violating a clearly defined and written driving covenant? If not, would it help to develop one together?**

2. **In what ways are your expectations for your teenager's use of the car reasonable? In what ways are they unreasonable? Does your teenager agree with your answers to these questions?**

3. **What are the natural consequences of your teenager's misuse of driving privileges likely to be?**

4. **Do you have the leverage to impose logical consequences for misuse of driving privileges? Can you, for instance, revoke the use of the car or even his driver's license?**

DATING

Of all of the issues in this chapter the issue of dating is likely to be the one that causes the most anguish. There is so much at stake. The questions that surround the areas of dating and sexual standards are often areas of non-communication in Christian homes. This is ironic in light of all the information on sexuality in Scriptures and the freedom Christ has given us from the cultural roles of our society.

There is not room in this chapter to deal with the topic of standards of sexual behavior. May we suggest the following excellent resources: **Preparing Youth for Dating, Courtship, and Marriage,** by Norman Wright and Marvin Inmon (Harvest House Publishers, 1978); **Sex and the Bible**, a cassette 2-pack by Norman Wright (Denver, Co.: Christian Marriage Enrichment, 1975); **A Love Story** by Tim Stafford (Zondervan, 1977). There are many other helpful resources in Christian bookstores as well.

It is important to have reviewed some of these resources before your chidren become teenagers so that you can remain open to their questions. If teenagers feel that their parents are not defensive of questions in an area such as sexuality they may communicate with their parents even when they're in trouble. But maybe some of those questions have already come up. Maybe you've already communicated anxiety when asked questions dealing with sex. It is **not** too late. At least you can be thankful that your teenager asked you these questions instead of someone outside your home. An excellent answer to a son or daughter's question is ''I don't know, but let's find out together. O,K.?'' The research you do separately or together can be an adventure for both of you and the communication of your results to each other may open up communication in other areas of life as well.

Dating is a cultural phenomenon that is rather recent in its present form and is changing as our culture changes. Believe it or not, it is possible to find a partner and get married without ever dating. People in other cultures do it all the time. So the whole role of dating needs to be discussed as a family. Some key questions you can think about together follow.

As in dialing and driving you might find a dating covenant to be most helpful. If you decide to use one, remember to develop the covenant together **with** your teenagers, not for them.

WHAT DO YOU THINK?

1. **What do each of you understand the objectives of dating to be?**

2. **What are your expectations of dating behavior? For example, is the guy expected to see how far he can go sexually? Is the girl supposed to be the one to decide on limits? Who is expected to decide what time to be home?**

3. **What qualities does your teenager have to offer a person he or she might date?**

4. **How does a girl pick her dates? Should she be passive and wait for a guy to ask her out? Why?**

5. What qualities do you look for in the person your teenager dates?

6. At what age do you feel various types of dating activity are appropriate; for instance first double, first single, formal and informal? Have you discussed these?

_____

_____

WHAT'S YOUR PLAN?

1. Which of the issues in this chapter is nearest to issues your family faces? Please pick one.

2. What suggestions for solving the issues in the

chapter were most appropriate to the issues you deal with?

3. Which suggestions would help most in the long run? — In the short run?

4. Which suggestions would be easiest to implement?

5. Is a combination of suggestions most appropriate? Which?

6. What will you try first?

7. **How will you know when this suggestion is either successful or replaceable by another suggestion?**

FOOTNOTE

1. Arthur J. DeJong, **Making It To Adulthood** (Philadelphia: Westminster, 1972), p. 45.

CHAPTER XII

Responsibility

If any signpost marks the beginning of adulthood it is the assumption of responsibility. Parents envy other parents whose teenagers seem to be more responsible than their own. Teenagers seem to want responsibility in some areas, like staying out later at night, taking trips on weekends with their friends, use of the family car or a car of their own, but not others like paying some of the monthly bills, helping little brother through school or the upkeep of the house and yard.

What is responsibility? Is it an innate quality inherited from parents? Is it born of adversity? Is it the same thing as self-discipline? Responsibility is defined differently by different people. We would like to suggest that responsibility is an ability to respond maturely. It is not quite the same as maturity because very young children can sometimes be responsible. But as people are given responsibility they tend to mature. Responsibility is not quite the same as self-discipline because very self-disciplined people can act irresponsibly sometimes and impulsive people can often be very responsible.

How are people, especially teenagers given responsibility? If we give a teenager a job to see through to completion have we given him responsibility? If he messes up, we say he was not very responsible. Sometimes responsibility is equated with duty, and sometimes it is the name given a character quality by which we describe a person.

One of the developmental tasks of teenagers is to become independent. Doing so inevitably transfers the power of making decisions into their hands. Is this responsibility? Or is responsibility the ability to make good decisions? If so, are good decisions the ones that agree with a parent's opinions or can a teenager make good decisions that conflict with his parents' decisions?

Can responsibility be taught? If so, how does a parent teach responsibility? Is responsibility more caught than taught? If so can we set up a climate tht is conducive to the "catching" of responsibility?

Three important factors in the growth of responsibility in young people are: 1) Development from dependence to independence; 2) Development in discipline from parental discipline to self-discipline; 3) The relationship between growth in the first two factors and parental expectations. [1]

Psychologists Erik Erickson and Robert Havinghurst describe the "developmental task" adolescents have as developing independence. In our society, junior high young people are dependent on their parents for almost everything. Money to buy clothes, records, anything else comes from their parents. They are dependent for transportation to any place out of bicycle or skateboard range. They have no choice about going to school, not legally anyway. By the time they are in college, young people can hold jobs and earn their own money. Most collegians have their driver's licenses and many have their own cars. They date and decide when the dates will end. They have made choices of their own about school, careers, and many other important decisions.

WHAT DO YOU THINK?

1. **How far have your teenagers come in their developmental tasks of growing independence? The point at the left end of the line below represents the dependence your teenagers had when they began seventh grade, and the point at the right when they are 20 years old. Put their initial on the line at the point of growth you think they each are at presently.**

._____.

DEPENDENCE   **INDEPENDENCE**

2. **See if your spouse agrees with you. If not, communicate till you agree with each other.**

While growing independence is an expectation most parents have for their teenagers, another factor that makes growing independence easier for most parents to handle is growth in self-discipline. Most junior high young people are motivated by parental discipline and the threat of negative consequences to any behaviors that are not self-gratifying. By the time young people are in college, parents hope they will be self-disciplined enough to "do what they have to do" on their own. Clues that a teenager is growing in self-discipline are his care of his room and clothes, discharge of his family duties without reminders, keeping his word, especially about return times on dates, and especially the kinds of choices he makes.

WHAT DO YOU THINK?

1. As you did with dependence-independence, put your teenagers' initials on the line below to indicate their growth in self-discipline.

._____.

PARENTAL DISCIPLINE   SELF-DISCIPLINE

Growth in independence and in self-discipline are interrelated in the relationship of parents and teenagers. Most parents will allow increasing independence quite readily if they feel that their teenagers are ready for it. So parents are primarily concerned about growth in self-discipline. On the other hand most teenagers are less concerned about their growth in self-discipline than the independence they see their peers attaining and feel they themselves need.

In the graph below you have growth in independence represented on the horizontal line and growth in self-discipline represented on the vertical line. If a teenager is growing just as fast in self-discipline as in independence, his development of what we will call responsibility will be a 45 degree line. The parental expectation line represents parents who expect their teenager to grow in self-discipline first, then independence will be granted.

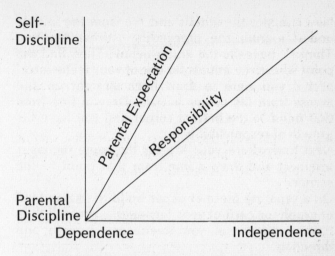

In some homes teenagers are growing in independence much quicker than in self-discipline. Their line of responsibility would be more horizontal than the one in the graph above. In some homes the parental expectation line and the responsibility line might be quite close or even the same line. In other homes these lines may be far apart. The distance between these two lines is a good measure of tension in a home.

WHAT DO YOU THINK?

1. On the independence and self-discipline lines in the preceding two "What Do You Think?" sections, add X's representing where you expect your young people should be in their growing independence and self-discipline. Are these X's at the same point as the teenagers' initials? In most families there is some distance between the initials and the X's.

2. Now transfer the initials and X's from the initials and X's from the preceeding "What Do You Think?" boxes to the graph below. Then find the point where the initials for one of your teens intersect if you were to draw lines straight up and across from his or her initials. Draw a line from that point to the bottom corner and you have his growth of responsibility.
3. Next find where your X's for the same teenager intersect and draw a line from that point to the corner.
4. On a separate piece of paper build the same kind of graph for each of your teenagers. You will then have a picture of your teenagers' growth and direction.

Self-
Discipline

Parental
Discipline

Dependence   Independence

Now that you have a picture of your teenagers' growth in responsibility, how do you respond? One distinction that needs to be made is the difference between self-discipline and conformity. Many parents equate their teenagers' self-discipline with conformity to their own opinions. If a teenager holds an opinion that is different from his parents, he may not be allowed the independence he needs because his parents don't trust him. Here is where conflict and tension often begin and need to be discussed. Parents can do two things—1) respect their teenager's different opinions while questioning them and 2) build a climate that encourages growing responsibility.

BUILD A CLIMATE

Some teenagers seem to learn responsibility faster than others. They seem to be in a climate that fosters growth. You might check the climate for growth in responsibility around your home against the following conditions. If these conditions are met, development of responsibility is more likely to occur than if they are ignored.

Condition 1. Encourage personal exploration and discovery. You can prompt exploration by providing your teenagers with the resources for exploration in areas they already show an interest. If your teenager is into auto mechanics, you might buy him a car that needs a new engine and the parts rather than buying him a new car. If he has questions about God or your church, get him into books and tapes that discuss these issues.

Keep asking questions as well, and avoid quick answers. "Let's find out" is not always satisfying, but encourages exploration far more than does an immediate opinion, even if the opinion is the "right" answer.

Condition 2. Encourage individual differences. Your teenagers are unique individuals. When they are stereotyped or pigeonholed they tend to live up to the stereotypes. This may make them more predictable, but they become less responsible. Teenagers compare themselves to each other enough. Encouraging a young person to "be more like your brother" usually backfires anyway. But parents can encourage their teenagers to express **themselves**, especially if their ideas and behaviors are copies of older brothers' or sisters' ideas or behaviors.

Condition 3. Encourage mistakes as well as excellence. This doesn't just mean that when a teenager makes a mistake we encourage him to try again. It means we encourage young people to learn by trial and error.

Parents are often so success and excellence oriented that their teenagers won't try a new idea or behavior for fear of failure. the parent who is or has been successful himself is especially likely to put this kind of pressure on his teenager. This parent acts on the need to be right or correct and usually snatches responsibility from his teenager just about the time the teenager would have failed. By so doing, the parent avoids watching his teenager make a mistake, but he creates a limiting and threatening condition for learning responsibility. When a teenager can expect to be penalized or punished this way for making mistakes, his freedom and willingness to make choices are severely handicapped.

If parents can show their teenagers that mistakes

are human, often necessary to growth, a way of learning, and in most cases not earth-shaking, teenagers can experiment with responsibility and grow.

Condition 4. Encourage the tolerance of ambiguity. Often responsible behavior has more than one option. Rarely is there only "one responsible solution." So when facing problems it is helpful to teenagers if parents are open to several alternatives. In fact, if parents can make time to explore many alternatives with their teenagers, young people will most often choose a responsible course of action.

Since adolescents are dealing with conflicting needs, drives, opinions and impulses, they are often stymied and immobolized by these conflicting desires and values. If they can learn to tolerate ambiguity, they can respond to conflict and avoid immobilization. This develops responsibility readily, especially when parents can handle adolescent mistakes.

Condition 5. Encourage cooperation and collaboration. Responsibility usually involves several people in interrelationship. Parents sometimes discourage responsibility by overdelegating. Each duty becomes part of a pattern of expectations, and a teenager sees only his duties and fails to consider the things that need to be done that haven't been assigned. Working together as parent and teenager on routine duties as well as on special obligations that come up will encourage responsibility.

Condition 6. Encourage personal openness. When a teenager feels shame or rejection for the way he has behaved, he tends to conceal himself, especially his emotions, from his parents. Pretty soon he gets out of touch with himself as he begins to conceal him-

self from himself. It is at this point that many teenagers get into alcohol and dope.

Parents can encourage personal openness by being
open themselves. We are better models for our teenagers if we admit our shortcomings, failures, and
sins and deal with them openly, than if we put on a
pretense of perfection. We help our teenagers "get it
together" by letting them know we are "getting it
together" rather than pretending we've "got it
together."

Condition 7. Encourage acceptance. We encourage
acceptance the same way we encourage personal
openness—by being what we want to encourage. The
teenager who is busy defending himself, even to
himself, is not free to grow in responsibility. If a
teenager feels unaccepted, just as he is, he finds it
difficult to accept himself. He may decide he needs to
change but he cannot because prior changes have led
to his present state of being unaccepted. God accepts
us "just as we are" when we come to Him. This is
our model for relationships with our teenagers.

Acceptance allows for growth because it gives a
teenager a safe platform from which to launch out
into new responsibilities.

Condition 8. Encourage respect. Responsibility is
more readily accepted by teenagers who respect
themselves than by teenagers who have little self-
respect. Since mutual respect is so basic to self-
respect by being open and honest and by respecting
our teenagers. Parents don't have to be perfect to be
respected, we will be respected by our teenagers if
we're open, honest and loving.

Our respect as parents for our teenagers, even
when they don't respect themselves will enable them

to take on responsibilities even when they are afraid to. In doing so, they will prove themselves to themselves and thereby gain self-respect. 2

WHAT IS YOUR PLAN?

1. Which of the eight conditions for building a climate or responsibility are strongest in your home? You might discuss with your spouse how you have built this climate in the past.
2. Which condition is hardest for you to understand its meaning or how to implement? This is probably the one you need to work on first. Start by brainstorming with your spouse ways you can be more encouraging in this condition.
3. Find out how your teenagers see themselves in their growth in responsibility by making up a graph for each of them and having them estimate how independent and self-disciplined they are. Graph their line or responsibility and compare it with the one you made for them. Are they close? You are likely to have lots of communication started by this comparison.
4. Review the chapter titles at the beginning of this book to build a priority list of things to work on. We hope you have already found practical helps and that you will find many more ways to build communication—the key to your teenagers.

FOOTNOTES

1. See Rex Johnson, "Middle Adolescence" in Roy B. Zuck & Warren S. Benson, **Youth Education in the Church** (Chicago: Moody 1978), pp. 132-133.
2. These conditions are adapted from an informal paper by John Castanha and Ronald R. Coryell for a course in Management Training for the Security Pacific Bank in California, then adapted by Rex Johnson in his book, **Ways to Plan and Organize Your Sunday School Youth** (Glendale, California: Regal, 1972), pp. 97-101.

Other Good
Harvest House Reading

COMMUNICATION—KEY TO YOUR PARENTS
by *Rex Johnson*

This guide teaches teenagers to rebuild the patterns of communication with their family.

TEENAGERS: PARENTAL GUIDANCE SUGGESTED
by *Rich Wilkerson*

With dynamic impact, well-known youth speaker Rich Wilkerson has captured for every sincere parent the secrets of achieving a fulfilling relationship with his teen. Honest answers for the tough issues we face with our children. Formerly *Hold Me While You Let Me Go*.

PARENTS IN CONTROL
Bringing Out the Best in Your Children
by *David Rice*

Getting your children under control is not as difficult as it might seem. *Parents in Control* explores: 1) How do parents get out of control? and 2) How to bring out the best in your child. Written for every parent, whether single or married, *Parents in Control* combines insight with a "nuts and bolts" approach to solving family problems.

THE FINAL CRY
by *Greg Laurie*

There is an epidemic sweeping our country today that is claiming the lives of young people at an alarming rate. It's the epidemic of teenage suicide. Last year over 6,000 teenagers killed themselves and over 600,000 tried! Each day there is a suicide attempt at the rate of one per minute. Greg Laurie takes a powerful look at the reasons behind teen suicide and the hope and help that the church must offer to young people desperate for answers. A thirty-minute video is also available.

GOD'S DESIGN FOR CHRISTIAN DATING
by *Greg Laurie*

In the midst of conflicting worldly standards, it is still possible to find and fulfill God's design for exciting relationships with the opposite sex. Offering godly counsel with touches of humor, Greg gives the "how-to" of healthy dating.